Constants of Delightful Worship

Constants of Delightful Worship

Praising One True God with Need and Thanksgiving

A biblical reference to current expectations

Dan Eze

iUniverse, Inc.
Bloomington

Constants of Delightful Worship
Praising One True God with Need and Thanksgiving

iUniverse books may be ordered through booksellers or by contacting:

iUniverse
1663 Liberty Drive
Bloomington, IN 47403
www.iuniverse.com
1-800-Authors (1-800-288-4677)

Because of the dynamic nature of the Internet, any web addresses or links contained in this book may have changed since publication and may no longer be valid. The views expressed in this work are solely those of the author and do not necessarily reflect the views of the publisher, and the publisher hereby disclaims any responsibility for them.

Any people depicted in stock imagery provided by Thinkstock are models, and such images are being used for illustrative purposes only.

Certain stock imagery © Thinkstock.

ISBN: 978-1-4620-2881-8 (sc)
ISBN: 978-1-4620-2883-2 (hc)
ISBN: 978-1-4620-2882-5 (e)

Printed in the United States of America

iUniverse rev. date: 06/24/2011

Contents

Introduction

God's presence is the most significant element of worship. God's presence and humanity's connection to His activity establishes the reason to worship Him on a daily basis. God, the creator, is the fundamental explanation both to humanity's existence and to the created universe.[1] In honor of humanity, created in His image, God formed the substance of the created universe to support humanity's dwelling.

You, like everyone else, are God's replica; nothing on Earth represents God more than you do. You represent God in all aspects of ideal life on Earth. Your life's purpose is centered on God's plan. These realities, which are the base of the spiritual system, deserve your attention. Every individual has the inner consciousness that proves that God is real, despite the protest of those who deny His being.

Let's examine genetic material as an analogy. Your DNA is patent proof of your biological origin, indicating that part of your ancestral parents exists in you. Through DNA, you believe that part of your parents and great-grandparents will live on through you and your children's children. That you share traits with your ancestors,

---

1   Gen. 1

however, does not form the basis for denying that you and your ancestors are separate individuals.

God is in our makeup, just as DNA is; the importance of accepting yourself as the image of God is hardly overrated. He created us in His image, making our spirits a reflection of His nature; much like our genetic material reflects our human nature.

The creation story in the book of Genesis implies that humanity owes its existence to the one true God. The invisible power advancing humanity's existence is not something that any earthly wisdom can fully explain. The power is divine and exists in utmost realism. It is no stretch to live in ways to please God. By pleasing God daily, we will, in practice, be the people that He created us to be, and thereby, we will find true happiness.

If you do not believe in God and therefore do not accept yourself as being created in His image, you may not understand the evil mindset fighting to own you. The ideas that support denying God are the devil's practical jokes. The unfortunate thing about the joke is that it confuses those who admire Satan's work to take him serious. People who do not believe in God's salvation tend to deny God's existence because they prefer to adore only the pleasures of life.

As it lacks the touch of the Spirit, the self-belief of those who do not believe in God is an illusory tale. Spiritual truth empowers the human conscience to stand up for righteousness against wrong ideas. No life lived outside the influence of the Holy Spirit is worth living. Do not allow your life to be filled with fantasy; if you do, you may take nothing but unrealizable dreams out of this world.

Misery and languishment are apparent realities in this life. The rich and the poor suffer; all people share the bitterness of life's troubles. We need wisdom that is more than this world can offer to counter the emptiness of life. According to the Book of Ecclesiastes, one may do his or her works diligently and be "successful," but the assumed success does not guarantee a hope that goes beyond death.

We came into this world with nothing; regardless of our material and intellectual success, we leave with nothing. Death is the ultimate equalizer of all people, and work done with the wrong attitude leads to emptiness. Two scriptures make this point clearly:

Naked I come and naked I will depart.[2]

To the ones who come after me, I must leave one day all of the things, which I have toiled for under the sun.[3]

Wisdom determines real success and makes room for true happiness. The cure to emptiness is to center one's life on God. The paradigm by which to measure life is not one of despair and vanity; rather, it is one of our understanding of life's true purpose. We must not build our lives on perishable pursuits but on the solid foundation that is God. Achieving spiritual purpose is life's reward. Time spent on Earth is not literally a matter of "soldier go, soldier come." To say it is meaningless to spend time on Earth is to believe that life is solely material. The dead are often forgotten and their legacies become a trace on the wind. The purpose of living is to worship God, for if you lack the true essence of worship, your despair will increase.

Humanity's criminal mind affects all of creation in similar ways. The problem is serious in that we perceive the damage that results from this criminality through earthly priorities, which differ from spiritual priorities. Humanity is in a state of serious moral decline; ironically humanity adopts misery as a way of life. We read in Matthew,

"Take my yoke upon you and follow me," Jesus invites you.

---

2   Job 1:21

3   Eccles. 2:17–23

"I am gentle and humble in heart, and you will find rest for your soul.
For, my yoke is easy and my burden is light." [4]

When we examine the vast atmosphere of misconduct influencing many people to move toward spiritual death, we see that it is understandable that the Church pulpit is never enough to talk God's sense into the heart of a perishing majority. As pastor, I assume the responsibility through all possible means and beckon the world to adopt the optimal approach to worshipping God. We must bear in mind that the only souvenir a believer may take to meet with God in heaven is other believers.

In writing this book, I used the biblical teachings about worship to create a clearer and more adequate understanding of the issue as it concerns our salvation. A faction of public opinion often misinterprets worship to include only what we do on Sunday morning during a church service rather than a way of living our daily lives in God. *Constants of Delightful Worship* will help you to better understand the nature of God within the concept of worship and will show you how incorporating delightful worship into your daily life can improve your relationship with God in particular ways.

Delightful Worship highlights the historical path of theology, along with present-day problems that hamper worship. It emphasizes the unity found in a combination of worshipfulness, Bible teaching ministry, and Bible study method. Readers can refer to the Bible throughout the book. Cross-references to passages in the Bible will help you verify each of the points. *Delightful Worship*, thereby, provides guidance to further study for virtually every subject. The observations, hopefully, will help you to facilitate your life and ministry.

---

4   Matt. 11:29–30

To help Christians maintain honor, I outlined a strategy for maintaining a good spiritual life in my book, *Intimacy with God*. Here, I followed a similar pathway in calling your attention to the important benefits of having a delightful, worshipful relationship with God. My writings are not intended for academic exercise. I consider the Holy Spirit revival the most important soul-benefiting exercise of any Bible study. The Holy Spirit inspired the authors of the Bible, and we can receive inspiration from this same Spirit by studying the Bible. My primary aim is to strengthen souls through this inspiration. It is my earnest desire that, by reading this book, you will come to terms with the true meaning of worship and help spread the word about its spiritual and material benefit. May the world, in mystification, know the truth and be freed by the knowledge.[5]

Worship does not solely involve going to church on Sunday morning; nor is it confined to praying alone or with family members in the morning, before meals, and in late evening before bedtime. Worship is not merely the joy of weekday prayer meetings, finding time to study the Bible, and giving charity. Worship constitutes living your daily life in God. A good worship practice reflects on everything that one does. Your worship should involve your career, your day-to-day relationships with people, your spiritual and mental standing, your mood, and the manner in which you come and go.

Worship is not about any*one* or any*thing* else but God, whose Spirit sheds light on us; our conduct should honor Him. One must not worship according to his or her personal desires; God's law, not the rule of any human condition, moderates worship. God's law is the basis for individual and corporate[6] day-to-day godliness. Every community has moral obligations as a body of people united in

---

5   John 8:32

6   *Corporate* refers to a unified body of people—a group often united in worship.

worship. We should not neglect to do and to share good things with others; for with such sacrifices God is pleased.[7]

> *God's truth is not in words taught by earthly wisdom, but in words taught by the Holy Spirit who expresses spiritual truth in spiritual words. The man without the Spirit does not accept the things that come from the Spirit of God, for they are foolishness to him, and he cannot understand them, because they are spiritually discerned. The spiritual man makes judgments about all things, but he himself is not subject to any man's judgment. For who has known the mind of the Lord that He may instruct him? But we have the mind of Christ.*[8]

The mind of Christ in this passage, which "we have," allows us to search for answers during periods of spiritual difficulty so that we may understand God's purpose and follow His lead. Silence and self-mindedness are inexcusable.

We read in Proverbs,

> *If you falter in times of trouble, how small is your strength. Rescue those being led away to death; and hold back those staggering toward slaughter. If you say, "But we knew nothing about this," does not He who weighs the heart perceive it? Does not He who guards your life know it? Will He not repay each person according to what he has done?*[9]

You are part of God's communication with the world; you should alert yourself to this opportunity to communicate on His

---

7   Heb. 13: 15 -16

8   1 Cor. 2:13–16

9   Prov. 24:10–12

behalf and proclaim the benefits of delightful worship. The Holy Spirit motivates His Church to identify worship in oneness of God. Here, the psalmist speaks well of priests whose strength of character brings people to God's temple (the temple worship of the Almighty God is in celebration of His universal reign):

Come let us sing for joy to the Lord; let us shout aloud to the Rock of our salvation. Let us come before Him with thanksgiving, and extol Him with music and song. For the Lord is the great God, the great King above all gods, and there is no corner of the universe that is not in His hand. Come let us bow down in worship, let us kneel before the Lord our Maker; for He is our God, and we are the people of His pasture; the flock under His care.[10]

Because Jesus Christ died on the Cross of Calvary, the curtain protecting the holiest part of the temple split; and from then on, whoever worshiped God in His presence could do so without fear of death. The event was a miracle by which God showed Himself to be the best friend any sinner could have. Jesus' death and resurrection is an appealing event—it has the opportunity to reunite humanity with God. Alone, we do not have the power to attain true happiness because we have ulterior motives. Without God, searching for satisfaction is a lost cause, but a life of delightful worship provides contentment. May God be gracious to us and make His presence shine on us; may His ways be known on Earth and His salvation among nations. May all people praise Him; and may the nations rejoice and sing for joy.[11]

---

10   Ps. 95:1–7

11   Ps. 67

The desire to be closer to God is a prelude to praise and worship; the latter results in the gift of God's presence on a daily basis. Moses said to the Lord,

> *If your presence does not go with us, do not send us up from here. How will anyone know that your people and I have found grace in your sight, except you go with us? What else will distinguish me and your people from all the other people on the face of the earth?*[12]

God's presence requires holiness; the functioning of the Holy Spirit unites all people in God. The Holy Spirit's revival of the new covenant is simply the new dimension of worship as dictated by that of the old covenant. In flesh and spirit, God is seeking godly offspring. The things that God has commanded are neither too difficult nor beyond any person's reach.

> *It is not up in heaven, so that you have to ask, "Who will ascend into heaven to get it and proclaim it to us so we may obey it?" Nor is it beyond the sea, so that you have to ask, "Who will cross the sea to get it and proclaim it to us so we may obey it?" No, the word is very near to you; it is in your mouth and in your heart, so you may obey it.*[13]

Do not neglect your responsibilities or allow what is convenient to rule you. Prioritizing things other than doing God's work is easy. But God wants you to follow through and build up His kingdom. Set your heart on what is right and adhere to that course. The more you delightfully worship God, the more you will appreciate God's loving kindness.

---

12   Exod. 33:15–16
13   Deut. 30:12–14

For the secret things belong to the Lord, our God, but the things revealed belong to us and to our children forever, that we may follow all the words of His law.[14]

It is my hope that reading this book will stimulate in you a new attitude toward God.

---

14   Deut. 29:29

My heart on a new age[15]

When my heart turns to a new age, happier and stronger in spirit I become. The older I am, the more I learn to judge myself by myself. Seeing my step toward spiritual maturity, I realize the past is like shadow on the evening sunlight.

When my heart turns to a new age, behold I look different. I witness my wishes drift away from where they once stood. My fascination drifts toward the future while I hold onto the present. The present is faith, and the future is God's hand at work.

So I teach my eyes to see beyond the rivers of the past that I may dwell in the realm of a living hope, which is the present. Every minute brings me closer to the future and moves me further away from the ugly faces of the past that chase after me. The present struggle is about realizing the great happiness of the future. I was nearly consumed by foolishness when I did not get hold of the Spirit in managing the seasons that turned ugly. Now that I am under His influence, gladly hopelessness is defeated.

Two kinds of experience allow me to learn. I can learn from the past by having lived the experience and from both past and present without living the experience. To learn from the past is to help the present form a better future. Inspiration gives me the confidence to find true goodness.

If your desire in Christ is problematic, take courage in God's love and fight on. His Spirit drives the wheel of every soul that believes in Him. In Him, you shall surely rejoice.

---

15   An excerpt from my poem, "especially for you"

Chapter 1

~~~

Signs of Cain and Abel

God's children will inherit the heavenly kingdom, and the only way to enter the kingdom is through righteously worshipping Him. Jesus Christ called God's kingdom His father's house, where He has gone to prepare a place for the faithful. Jesus is very certain about the many rooms in His father's house, so much so that He told His disciples,

If it were not so, I would have told you.[16]

The trials and temptations of this life, both those that are foreseeable and those that are unforeseeable, greatly hinder our spiritual progress. This concern compelled Jesus to say,

Watch and pray.[17]

---

16   John 14:2
17   Matt. 26:41

From the Gospel's standpoint, you are not required to be a good person in order to be a true worshipper of God. Everyone was born of sin[18], and we all struggle with the effect. The grace of God's salvation protects your present decision to offer your life to Jesus Christ against failures of the past. God wants you to come to Him with your struggles and doubts. His answer may not always be what you expect, but God will sustain you by revealing Himself to you. Trust in God will lead you to quiet hope, not bitter retirement. Hope means going beyond your unpleasant daily experience to the joy of knowing God. You will improve spiritually if you live daily by the incorruptible breath of God's Spirit.

The Holy Spirit provides rebirth, laying the groundwork for inner purity and hope for the future. The process of rebirth acts as a catalyst for erasing an ugly past and a worrisome present. The mission of salvation is not the result of human goodness but of human failure. God's purpose is redemption, and human failure is no excuse; rather, it is a reality. True believers live by trusting in God, not by the benefits that they may experience in this life. Be assured that God is in control of this world, in spite of the apparent triumph of evil.

Satan's basic goal is to counterfeit God's good works; this has been his prized ambition ever since he claimed independence and presumed himself to be "like the Most High."[19] With the rebel angels on his side, Satan formed a kingdom of his own—a counterfeit kingdom of darkness designed to lure men and women to abandon their worship of God. Satan's counterfeiting effort is his most

---

18   "Surely I was sinful at birth, sinful from the time my mother conceived me" (Ps. 51:5).

    "How then can a man be righteous before God? How can one born of woman be pure? If even the moon is not bright and the stars are not pure in His eyes, how much less man, who is but a maggot, a son of man who is only a worm" (Job 25:4–6).

19   Isa. 14:14

effective ploy; the more closely he can imitate God's work, the less likely people will be inclined to seek God or pursue His will.

The kingdom of darkness exists through voluntary evil forces, and God temporally allows it to exist as a tempting option for all moral creatures in their exercise of moral freedom. God does not overlook any activity of this world. He will rule this world with perfect justice. At the moment, the good Christian does not exist because the struggle isn't finished. Jesus rejected the title "good" when He said,

Why do you call me good? No one is good, but God alone.[20]

Jesus seems to imply that true goodness is the prerogative of God alone. There is no perfection except in God. You are essentially required to commit yourself to God through delightful worship in order to revive the influence of the Holy Spirit daily. You will surely improve yourself by exercising this form of true goodness. His grace redeems those who believe in His word, and by His mercies, the believer's new birth grows daily to living faith.[21]

As for you, you were dead in your transgressions and sin, in which you used to live when you followed the ways of this world, and the ruler of the kingdom of the air, the spirit who is now at work in those who are disobedient. All of us also lived among them at one time, gratifying the cravings of our sinful nature and following its desires and thoughts. Like the rest, we were by nature objects of wrath. But because of His great love for us, God, who is rich in mercy, made us alive with Christ even when we were dead in transgressions; it is by grace that you are saved.[22]

---

20   Mark 10:18
21   1 Peter 1:3
22   Eph. 2:1–5

The apostle Paul reminds all Christians about the reality of personal sin, from which Jesus redeems every one of us. You must not forget the past from which Jesus saved you. This is not to say that you should remain in bondage of the past; however, the memory of His sacrifice for your salvation demands your gratitude.

Worshipping with an attitude that allows you to consider yourself better or worse than anyone else is wrong, for in doing so, you are setting your judgment above that of God. God loves us even when we fail Him, but He also loves other people, including those who are not of our group and background. Improving your worshipful relationship with God does not give you license to view either yourself or anyone else as "good," as this designation is for God alone. Whenever you perceive yourself as good, you will severely endanger your spiritual growth and hinder your relationship with people.

On a relative scale, no one is totally useless. Even unbelievers at times do good things; some are moral, kind, and law-abiding. But only God is perfect. It is essential that the process of revival by the Holy Spirit manifests in all aspect of your life. Having a true spirit of worship implies that you adjust your desire from time to time to always agree with the Holy Spirit. Worshippers of God are called righteous, not by themselves but by the righteousness of God.

Such confidence as this, is ours through Christ before God; not that we are competent in ourselves to claim anything for ourselves, but our competence comes from God. He has made us competent as ministers of a new covenant—not of the letter but of the Spirit; the letter kills, but the Spirit gives life.[23]

---

23   2 Cor. 3:4–6

A repentant heart transforms us, moving us toward goodness. The critical stage of transition is the struggle to believe in God's saving grace, which transforms biblical faith to personal faith. For one's spiritual growth to steadily occur, he or she must constantly revive in him or herself the process of repentance. Christian heritage comes with personal struggle and cannot be passed on with the same ease as a son may inherit his father's assets. The only reason for the Holy Spirit's revival is the presence of sin. Again, the privilege of God's righteousness does not provide us authority to despise anyone, despite the depth of many people's involvement in sin. Those who you despise by any circumstance can, in future, be better friends of God. The concept reflects the teaching of Jesus Christ when He told the Pharisees that He did not come to call the righteous ones but to call the sinners to repent.[24] Jesus was saying that the flow of God's consciousness is an important doorway to true goodness. The inherent consciousness of God separates humanity from beasts. Worship is obligatory to all who possess God's image:

> *You shall worship the Lord your God, and only Him you shall serve.*[25]

The Church and Worship
The sole purpose of assembling the Church is worship. A person joins the Church when he or she comes to agreement with the high calling of God in Jesus Christ. The Church did not start or grow by any human power and enthusiasm. We join the fellowship of the Church as the disciples were empowered by the Holy Spirit to engage the ministry. The Holy Spirit is the promised counselor sent by Jesus Christ to facilitate the Church's ultimate goal, which is

---

24   Matt. 9:13, Mark 2:17
25   Luke 4:8

worship.[26] The Church is the hope of upcoming world revival, and worship attracts God's love by revealing the consciousness of His supreme power.

Missionary work exists because true worship does not. Faulty worship is the reason behind missionary work. An ideal worshipper of the biblical God does not act in opposition to universal goodness. True worship acts to purify by incorporating a sinful soul into the fellowship of the Holy Spirit. The essence of the revival is reconciliation, which through Jesus Christ is the task of the Church.

The fellowship of the Church is one of the most fundamental realities of Christian faith. The Bible presents the Church as people of God—the community and body of Christ. Jesus Christ came to Earth to gather God's assembly—to call people from every corner of the Earth to manifest unity in honoring God.

Sunday morning worship involves unified prayers and praise. We cannot overestimate its usefulness in terms of finding peace with God. When we are assembled, keeping praise and worship forefront in our minds will help us remain always in the spirit of prayer. The true concept of worship is coherent with God's loving relationship with His children. By studying and following God's standard as they are laid out in the Bible, God's children can identify with those standard.

We must not forget, however, that not every worshipper is a true child of God. True children of God are those who truthfully attempt to follow His lead. Jesus proclaimed the coming of God's saving kingdom with His presence and triumphed over sin and Satan by being resurrected from the dead. Those who reject Jesus' claim will lose their place in the kingdom as a result of unbelief,

---

26   "When the Counselor comes, whom I will send to you from the Father, the Spirit of truth who goes out from the Father, He will testify about me. And you also must testify, for you have been with me from the beginning" (John 15:26–27).

whereas faithful believers will forever reign with Jesus Christ in God's heavenly presence.[27] The ingathering of the faithful is now; the exercise will last to the end of all things, when the gathered will finally be brought together as a people. The gathering of the Church is by no means geographically limited; rather, joins in one fellowship people of every nation and tribe.[28] For this reason the Church should not exclude from its membership anyone who credibly confesses the Lord Jesus as the Christ. As we read in John,

> For as many as they are who believes in Him, and have received Him, to those He gave the right to become children of God.[29]

This right is not granted according to natural descent; nor is it passed on through any human arrangement. Rather, it is an election of people born of God:

> If anyone is in Jesus Christ, he is a new creation; the old has gone, and behold the new has come. All this is from God, who reconciled us to Himself through Christ, and gave the ministry of reconciliation.[30]

God is hostile to sin, and therefore, He is detached from sinners. But when a person reconciles his or her sin by the Spirit of the Lord

---

27   "And if I go and prepare a place for you, I will come back and take you to be with me that you also may be where I am." (John 14:3).

28   "After this, I looked and there before me was a great multitude that no one could count, from every nation, tribe, people, and language standing before the throne and in front of the Lamb. They were wearing white robes and were holding palm branches in their hands and they cried out, 'Salvation belongs to our God who sits on the throne, and to the lamb'" (Rev. 7:9–10).

29   John 1:12

30   2 Cor. 5:17–18

Jesus Christ, the sinner ceases being God's enemy and a slave to sin. By detaching from deliberate wrongdoing, we are God's sons and daughters, freed and sanctified with the blood of Jesus Christ.[31] This adoption is the most gracious of the privileges that God offers us, and it should motivate the world to believe all of God's promises. By redeeming us from sin, Jesus takes away the fear of death, which separates us from the everlasting love of the Father.

Realizing that everyone, through repentance, is welcome to join God's divine family, the Church bears the task of helping everyone achieve God's forgiveness. Everyone ought to believe the Gospel; by believe each of us can become a person born of God.

Being born of God is not the same as a natural birth. Being born of God is a rebirth of spirit, wherein you enter into a new relationship with God and with the manner in which you worship Him. Being in this relationship will begin to overhaul your perception of this life. The process begins when you acknowledge God through obedience and faith. Obedience is a commitment, which God's people owe to Him as citizens of His divine kingdom. The services of obedience are based on love, and love provides the platform to test our knowledge of God.

In a more personal dimension, both your loyalty to God and your good relationships with other people are evidence of your unconditional love for God. However, the commandment to love one another, especially as brethren, is relatively new; this commandment came to us during the age of the New Testament. Jesus gave the commandment to love according to a new standard and motivation when He said,

> *A new commandment I give to you, that you love one another;*
> *as I have loved you, that you also love one another. By this*

---

31   "So you are no longer a slave, but a son; and since you are a son, God has made you also an heir" (Gal. 4:7).

all men will know that you are my disciples, if you love one another.[32]

Jesus speaks of bodily inconveniencing love, a practice that only those who are led by the Holy Spirit can truly cling to. Christian love is not the secular imitation of love embroiled with bodily warm feeling but good work revealing the actions of true goodness. In a true Christian sense, love is an attitude that accepts God's will from the standpoint of Jesus' example. Jesus gave His life for the sake of all people. By His example, we are challenged to adopt a lifestyle that benefits not only personal interest but also the commandments of God's special mercy. About God's commandments, we are told,

Impress them on your children. Talk about them when you sit at home, and when you walk along the road, when you lie down and when you get up. Tie them as symbols on your hands and bind them on your foreheads. Write them on the doorframes of your houses, and on your gates.[33]

If you truly love God and your neighbor, you will naturally obey the rest of the commandments, not worrying about what you should not do. Exercising biblical love is a positive way to walk on God's path.[34] Doing so adds to divine providence the grace that separates us from ungodliness.

---

32   John 13:34–35

33   Deut. 6:5–8

34   Lev. 19:18; "Love the Lord your God with all your heart, and with all your soul, and with your entire mind. This is the first and greatest commandment. And the second is like it, 'Love your neighbor as yourself.' All the Law and the Prophets hang on these two commandments" (Matt. 22:37–40).

The apostle Paul asks dangling Christians to fully reconcile with God:

Now then we are ambassadors for Christ as though God were pleading through us: we implore you on behalf of Christ to reconcile with God.[35]

Nothing about the Gospel made more sense to Paul than asking his listeners to adhere delightfully to worshipping the living God.

The Holy Spirit holds the Church together in divine lordship. No Church can function appropriately without a good system of spiritual worship, and in all Churches the congregation's relationship with God functions according to a pattern of worship. As the Spirit of truth, the Holy Spirit completes the revelation of scripture. As the Spirit of witness, He leads the Church in its mission. As the Spirit of life, He liberates the Church from sin and death. The Holy Spirit has uplifted His people by providing two opportunities with one concept.

Church is a holy temple—a place where God's people gather to worship God.[36] Consider, then, the worthiness of our human body, which the Bible perceives as the temple of the Holy Spirit. He whom we receive from God lives in us.[37]

---

35   2 Cor. 5:20

36   Isa. 56:7; "My house will be called a house of prayer for all nations" (Mark 11:17).

37   1 Cor. 6:19– 20; we are bought at a cost and, therefore, should honor God with our bodies. The apostle Paul calls on Christians to show their status in God by not offering any part of their bodies as instrument to sin but giving their bodies to righteousness. We were once dead in sin, but we are now alive in God through Jesus Christ.

You were included in Christ, when you heard the word of truth,
the Gospel of your salvation; having believed, you were marked
in Him with a seal, the promised Holy Spirit.[38]

This implies that our bodies are sacred with the Holy Spirit's presence. His presence makes worship an inside out exercise.

Christians whose worship diet has no theological ingredient are likely to suffer imbalanced growth, not developing maturity of mind. Good intentions can fall short when loving fellowship exists alone, providing no context for discipline. Without proper discipline that is preventive and corrective, the body can greatly damage the good intentions of the heart. Therefore, the apostle Paul said,

I urge you in view of God's mercy, to offer your bodies as living
sacrifices, holy and pleasing to God—this is your spiritual act
of worship. Do not conform any longer to the pattern of this
world, but be transformed by the renewing of your mind. Then
you will be able to test and approve what God's will is - His
good, pleasing, and perfect will.[39]

In Ephesians, we read,

Do not let any unwholesome talk come out of your mouths, but
only what is helpful for building others up according to their
needs, that it may benefit those who listen. And do not grieve
the Holy Spirit of God, with whom you were sealed for the
day of redemption. Get rid of all bitterness, rage and anger,
brawling and slander, along with every form of malice. Be kind

---

38   Eph. 1:13
39   Rom. 12:1–2

*and compassionate to one another, forgiving each other, just as
in Christ God forgave you.*"[40]

The Holy Spirit is a person and an influence; when He resides
within us, His power gives us the ability to resist sin and its desires.

If the purpose of the Church assembling together is, indeed, to
worship God, the gatherers must anticipate the experience of God's
special influence. If the gathering is of pure heart, the Holy Spirit's
presence guarantees that God will answer the worshippers' prayers
and grant miracles. The Bible recommends that every believer should
stay in the assembly in order to remain focused on Godly; together,
believers must constantly inspire to do good works and love one
another.[41] Jesus said,

*Where two or three come together in my name, there am I with
them.*[42]

Jesus Christ is present with those who are involved in proper,
disciplined, and spiritual functions of the Church, such as worshipping
with a pure heart and praying according to God's will.

He is not physically present amid the gathered saints, but His
Spirit provides hope that He will physically return to Earth as He
has promised. Jesus' resurrection from the dead thereby connects
believers, allowing them to forever partake in God's kingdom.[43]
Jesus has power over life and death. His Spirit gives the Church a
spiritual type of life, which death cannot conquer:

---

40   Eph. 4:29–32

41   "Let us consider one another in order to stir up love and good works,
not forsaking the assembling of ourselves together" (Heb. 10:24–25).

42   Matt. 18:20

43   "He who believes in me, though he may die, yet shall live again" (Heb.
10:24–25).

There is now no condemnation for those who are in Christ Jesus,
because through Christ Jesus the law of the Spirit life set all free
from the law of sin and death.[44]

Jesus died for one reason alone—love. Our love for one another must manifest itself in all works through integrity, and these works must include regular, consistent gatherings in His name. Love and unity among believers demonstrates the power of God's immense care. Love is the primary focus of worship, without which no one shall inherit the kingdom of God.

The pain of death is Christ's alone, but the benefit of an everlasting freedom belongs to all persons who trust in Him. The testimony of the Church should reflect the sincerity of faith, which accordingly is the assurance of the sanctifying power of Christ's blood. We see the fullness of our salvation in three essential ways—by recognizing what Christ has saved us from; by accepting His love, which He gives us freely; and finally, by accepting God's grace.

The Church, corporately and individually, must desire worship from God's standpoint. He provides a foretaste of glory in the Spirit of adoption. A life of delightful worship could reverse all your bad habits and memories. Once you fully step into this life, you will discover within yourselves other good qualities, some of which you may not have realized that you possessed. When put to the test and conditions of life ask people to either live or die for their faith, a secondhand Christianity is not worth much.

Heart and Worship
In Old Testament days, worship included sacrificial offering, rituals, and ceremonies. Individual burnt offerings were particularly popular among the earliest worshippers. Believers would make an offering to

---

44   Rom. 8:1

ask God for a good harvest at the beginning of the farming season or to give thanks for the harvest at the end of the season. God permitted animal sacrifices and burnt offerings. Purely figurative, these offerings served as mere symbol and shadow of the Messiah's offer.[45] In various occasions, especially at later ages, individual sacrifice was used as a means for appeasing God against sin. Priests performed burnt offerings, slaying lambs and doves in the temple as blood sacrifices in exchange for sins. People prepared fruits and vegetables as sacrificial thanksgiving.

The practice is different from that of the New Testament era, when believers inherited access to the Holy Spirit's influence as a gift from Jesus Christ. It is gratifying to know that the ultimate price of blood sacrifice has been paid in full. All individual and temple sacrifices of burnt offering have, therefore, ended. Jesus paid the ultimate price for sin, and no other sacrifice is required of anyone; we have only to believe in Jesus Christ and reflect that belief on a daily basis. Referring to the atonement for sin, Jesus said on the cross,

It is finished.[46]

The first illustration of sacrificial worship in the Bible is found in the story of Cain and Abel. The two brothers had the most ancient occupations of today's Middle East:

Abel kept flocks and Cain worked the soil.[47]

---

45   Heb. 10:11–12; "And every priest stands ministering daily and offering repeatedly the same sacrifices, which can never take away sins. But this Man, after He had offered one sacrifice for sins forever, sat down at the right hand of God. For by one offering He perfected forever those who are being sanctified" (Heb. 10:14).

46   John 19:30

47   Gen. 4:2

The fourth chapter in Genesis reveals the nature of burnt offerings by which Cain and Abel worshipped God. Abel offered fat portions from some of the firstborn of his flock, and God accepted the offer. Cain, on the other hand, offered some of the fruits of his farm produce, and God did not accept this offer. The Bible is not precise as to why God rejected Cain's offering. Perhaps Cain's attitude was the reason for the rejection.

The compelling outcome of these brothers' worship concerns motive, not substance. There is nothing from a spiritual standpoint to show that the substance of Cain's offering was inappropriate. The intention of worship is to honor God, but Cain and Abel were separated by their mind-sets. The brothers' hearts were, to God, the underlying and most significant factor. Substance is not the most important element of any worship; the heart is.

The heart is the human storehouse, where springs of thought evolve into action. The preacher, who is the author of the Book of Proverbs, calls the heart "the wellspring of life" and recommends that we guide our hearts with the word of God, swerving neither to the right nor to the left.[48] Our hearts dictate a great deal about how we live. If you keep your heart clean, your actions toward God will be good, and He will find your adoring thanksgiving acceptable.

How one accepts God's attributes reflects one's choices about the relationship he or she has with Him. This is true of all people. It was true when Cain and Abel made their offerings to God. If you follow the guidance the Bible gives about worship, you will realize that the emphasis is not ordinarily on the form of the offering. The brothers' willingness to offer sacrifice to God truly came from their hearts. Cain and Abel believed that God deserved to be honored with the fruits of their labor. Desiring to honor God, the brothers decided to

---

48   Prov. 4:23

offer Him sacrifice. However, how one should honor God and with what attitude then came into play, as it still does.

Cain and Abel may have been the first to experience God's judgment in terms of whether or not He would accept their way of worshipping Him, but they were certainly not the last. The internal battle to be totally committed and humbly obedient is a worrisome aspect of our daily worship. As a result of false piety, many ugly outcomes of our services to God are diminishing happiness in the world. We should exercise joyful hearts when we give to God and others because what we can give is the gift of God. For Cain and Abel, the individual judgment about what God deserved was verified by their offering, and this was why God rejected Cain's offering.

The story of Cain and Abel is a good insight into many worship attitudes. I am fascinated by meditation, and I use the practice to improve my worshipful relationship with God in a similar way that I offer my thoughts about times and events to enlighten Church audiences.

The story of Abel's worship bears witness to our ability to please God by means of material blessings and the appropriate mind-set. Abel demonstrates that a true worshipper must come to God with faith and present the sacrifice required of him, which only God can accept. No one can reach out to God from outside his or her heart. One's closeness to God depends on one's determination to close gaps. The Lord said,

You will seek me and find me when you seek me with all your heart.[49]

Possibly, Cain and Abel were not aware of these implications. Even so, God rejected Cain's offering to correct his attitude. Abel

---

49   Jer. 29:13

had a good desire to worship God and a delightful heart that backed up his attitude. Cain had also a good desire to worship God, but he used the wrong attitude. Cain's attitude did not agree with God's nature. A true worshipper of God must show through his or her attitude that he or she puts God first.

God is the loving father of all. He hates no one, but He is above everyone. God does not cause pain but heals the pain of sin when we let Him. Cain had the opportunity to change his attitude to reflect God's viewpoint, but he didn't. If Cain had been able to make this change, he would have been able to put before God a desirable offering. In direct contrast to the way Cain made his offering, Cain's heart would be the first offering to God, followed by the symbolic material portion of his offering.

Nevertheless, one's attempt to please God may not always resolve all one's outstanding defiance. Worship may result either in reproof or in God's loving approval. As imperfect beings, we ought to expect both reproof and blessing as outcomes of our worship. In some ways, we may see reproof as a blessing in disguise. Delightful worship by repeated effort results in spiritual growth. When God reproves us, the intended outcome is that we make amendments and do the right thing. Thus, the received reprimand unambiguously promotes our chance to further befriend God. The preacher said,

My son, do not despise the Lord's discipline and do not resent His rebuke, because the Lord disciplines those He loves as a father, the son he delights in.[50]

---

50   Prov. 3:11–12; "Blessed is the man whom God corrects; so do not despise the discipline of the Almighty. For He wounds, but He also binds up; He injures, but His hands also heal. From six calamities He will rescue you. In famine He will ransom you from death, and in battle from the stroke of the sword; you will be protected from the lash of the tongue, and need not to fear when destruction comes" (Job 5:17–21).

A positive attitude toward God will always enable you to see God's way as the best way. A time of affliction could be to you, as it is to virtually all believers, a time of increasing faith. An element of a good test is that it elevates our spiritual steps to higher ground.

We can examine more aspects of the patterns of our worship by exploring the story of Cain and Abel. There are many examples to it, but I can relate only a few of the examples in this episode. The Holy Spirit commands insight, and leaders of God's house are compelled to use His insight to modify many wavering worship habits.

The Holy Spirit models how we should conduct our everyday lives, and every Church member should be concerned with His teachings.

The Father, who asks that we delightfully worship Him, has predetermined that, if we do, He will reward us accordingly. Righteousness may not always determine prosperity, but the diverse gifts we receive do not divide us from one another. Each individual effort unites the Church as a functioning body.

However, it is useful to distinguish between the broad and restrictive meanings of worship as they apply to God. God may be honored with prayer and praise songs, as well as the bringing of donations. In a narrower sense, worship is pure adoration—the lifting up of the redeemed spirit toward God in contemplation of His holy perfection. The two concepts of worship require daily integrity and pure heart.

Perverse worship is the intent to make either one's self or someone or something else the subject of honor that properly belongs to God. Many spiritually dead and living Churches exist in our time, and many Cains and Abels worship in various places of worship. Spirits like Cain and Abel are active; those who follow Abel's example and defeat the spirit of perversion are constantly under the attack of Satan.

Satan's goal is to force the Church of Christ to bow down and worship him.[51] There is no doubt about the presence of demonic powers at work, seeking to mislead the Church. These are spirits of the Antichrist; they are rife with idolatry and occultism and produce counterfeits and devilish representation of the gifts of the Holy Spirit, such as false teaching.

The solution to Satan's attack is not to swing from one congregation of believers to another but to stand firm in the righteousness of God against falsehood. Worship is a spiritual exercise; God easily perceives any hypocrisy in a pattern of worship. Many worshippers are yet to amend their ways; like Cain, they somehow adore double standards. We must be gratefully that God raises people and groups to meet the concern of any particular time and place. We are individually responsible for our future in God, and we retain the ability to determine what that future is.

For our young ones—children growing up in the house of God—good parenting and ideal family value are the roots to their upbringing. Teaching children biblical narrative gives them moral lessons and aids them as they grow to find the right path to delightful worship.

Some parents and guardians may argue that there is not one way to child upbringing, but the biblical viewpoint is clear. The preacher said,

> *Bring up a child in the way he should go, and when he is old he will not depart from it.*[52]

Train a child in a morally excellent way and allow the child the opportunity to work out certain realities of life using his or her own

---

51   "Again the devil took Him to a very high mountain and showed Him all the kingdoms of the world and their splendor. 'All this I will give you,' he said, 'if you bow down and worship me'" (Matt. 4:8–9).

52   Prov. 22:6

sense and experience. You can incorporate important lessons into a child's memory when you train a child to pray, sing hymns and songs of praise, and memorize certain Bible stories. The exercise of singing hymns and songs of praise is part of the best religious education for children; it helps to develop their spiritual growth more rapidly and tends to tie them to Church for life.

Bringing up a child explicitly involves investing graciously in the child—providing refined wisdom and demonstrating the true meanings and examples of love, reverence, and discipline. To be able to do so presupposes the emotional and spiritual maturity of parents and guardians. Those who desire to teach good manners must lead the example.[53]

Delightful worship counts each day as the best day to lift up yourself to God through prayer and moral behavior. The daily path of delightful worship requires a type of struggle, the triumphant outcome of which is sufficiently satisfying. Being willing to let God be God is an excellent way to ensure that you do not deny yourself or anyone else His joy. To let the Spirit dwell fully in you is to live the experience of His full control. If His love fills your heart, you will willfully serve Him with every bit of your strength.[54]

If you take God away from a child, you have denied the child his or her most powerful moral tool for surviving life's hardships. Challenges of life will always be around, and sometimes, they will destroy people who are psychologically weak. But with God, there is always something left in people to safeguard them from hurting themselves and other people. By God's indwelling presence, servants of the Lord may rid themselves of the worrisome yoke of this life. In Him, we live to teach by good example.

---

53   "Those who are wise will shine like the brightness of the heavens, and those who lead many to righteousness, like the stars forever and ever" (Dan. 12:3).

54   Matt. 22:37; Deut. 6:5

In the Gospel, we find a fascinating story about the widow's mites. The message thereof meets the intent of this book and further illustrates the point about Cain's attitude. Jesus told the story from the Gospel through the apostle Mark.[55] Jesus and His disciples went to the temple for evening worship and sat opposite the place where offerings were collected. Jesus could see the crowd of worshippers putting their cash offerings in the temple's treasury. Many rich people threw in large amounts, but a poor widow came by and put in two very small copper coins. Afterward Jesus commended the poor widow before His disciples, saying,

This poor widow has put in more than all those who have given to the treasury.[56]

The poor widow gave the best that she could, and God recognized her offering more than those of the wealthy. He honored her more because she trusted God more. Her generosity and sacrifice contrasted to the way most worshippers use their riches and time in serving God. Quantity does not always constitute the best offering, but a good and generous heart will always do. Peevishly providing the Church with plenty of silver and gold is less worthy than the sacrifice of a sincere and gratifying heart. Jesus observed the amount of money that each donor gave *and* the donors' mind-sets. Your heart determines where you invest your love, and your attitude controls the value.

The implications of the stories about Cain and Abel and the widow's mites reflect experiences I have had from many perspectives. Some rich people call attention to their offering by making a great show of it. Jesus condemns the attitude as ungodly—a prideful

---

55   Mark 12:41–44
56   Mark 12:43

desire for prominence found among the scribes and the Pharisees. Such display of false piety misleads many good worshippers.

The present-day challenge in terms of false piety is particularly found among the pastoral leadership. I doubt if many Church leaderships take seriously poor Christians who happen to be spiritually efficient and heartfelt donors. Modern Church leadership, at most, does not consider spiritual riches above material wealth. The status quo views material poverty as criminal. The poor are neglected, regardless of their nonjudgmental attitude and spiritual loyalty to the Church. The "widow's mites" is a scenario that repeats on several fronts, but again and again, more Church leaders offer honor to higher donors. The tenet of today is the more you give, the more you are honored. Even when Church leaders don't express this notion openly, it is a psychological reality. Regard and respect exchange hands these days among the rich and the famous. The more one can afford to throw money around, the higher one is honored. If there is an argument that suggests the opposite as the case, it should cite poor Christians who are famous for their higher spiritual quality and a Church where front seats are set as dispensation for people like the poor widow.

The situation is unfortunate, and the likelihood is that special consideration is equated with money and undue favor, rather than with true commitment to God. The rich have no higher spiritual standing but money. It is appalling that the world's most popular preachers make friends among only the rich. Desire for indulgence is a twenty-first century, extremely serious attack on spirituality and a greater danger to the contemporary man of God. In a modern Church setting, everything about worship goes with money and fame. The success of a Church is determined by its outstanding wealth and the pastors fame, rather than by the spiritual well-being of the members. These are days when Church membership rolls may as well represent the money leadership expects per week's gathering.

Money is not evil, but the love of money is mentioned in the Bible as *a root of all kinds of evil.*[57] A restless desire for richness can easily subject one to great spiritual downfall. The gradual shift to a paradigm of wealth and pleasure against spirituality is damaging to our common relationship with God. According to the apostle Paul,

Some people, eager for money, have wandered from the faith, and have pierced themselves with many griefs.[58]

Offering was a tiny part of worship in the beginning days of the Church, and it was far less significant than holiness.[59] Holiness of the Church fulfills the Old Testament symbolism of ceremonial cleanliness by a moral purity fashioned of the Holy Spirit. But the process of time is changing all that as a result of less commitment to the Holy Spirit's influence. Money assumes the tendency to command our thoughts above the pursuit of holiness. The overriding influence of money is evidently working against the blooming of the essentials of worship. As the influence of money approaches the center stage of worship, inner brightness of spirit worship slips from God's power at work and monetary generosity takes precedence.

Modern worship, in particular, translates to beautiful facilities and fancy programs, rather than the true holiness of love. In God's worship, money should not have more influence than the necessity of money, and its influence should not disqualify the dignity of spiritual worship. Money alone does not indicate love in the heart. Offering is a unique function of worship and spells out the importance of God reigning in our heart, but spirit worship must command the lead. Whatever the offer, the most essential element is our attitude;

---

57   1 Tim. 6:10

58   1 Tim. 6:10

59   Acts 5:1–11; Ananias and Sapphire

an offer with the right attitude pleases God more than any element of worship fashioned by humanity.

Everything that Christians do should contribute to the knowledge of God. Money and service that requires money do not sum up the high elements of worship but may occasionally strike the right note. It is our rational response to God's mercy to dedicate our pockets to Him, but it is more important to dedicate our bodies and souls to His worship. No act of worship is more significant and spiritually rewarding than the act of consecrating our body to form part of our religious services to God. With the Holy Spirit, the Church understands offering as total commitment that translates soul, body, and substance. The process of worship is, thereby, not a single event; and likewise, spiritual worship is not merely a ritual activity. It is unsafe to work out a form of delightful worship based merely on going to Church and making donations. Recognizing that God's Spirit dwells in you may help you guard your spiritual life more than any other form of worship.

Those who grab earthly wealth through ungodly means fail to realize that God is not against prosperity. God created humanity to take charge of the earth. God said,

> *The fear and dread of you will fall upon all the beasts of the earth and all the birds of the air, upon every creature that moves along the ground, and upon all the fish of the sea; they are given into your hands. Everything that lives and moves will be food for you. Just as I gave you the green plants, I now give you everything.*[60]

Many people do not engage wisdom in decision making; if they did, they would realize they should not work against their own righteousness and future happiness. There is lack of good judgment

---

60   Gen. 9:2–3

on account of the majority because the common outlook has poor vision of God's purpose. Fear of losing control of life and the desire to influence people with resources cause unrighteous pursuit. Short-term happiness always leaves behind many problems. Those eager to be rich usually close their hearts and fail to recognize that God is the only security they need to be truly happy.

Allowing the cause of creation to coincide with your existence and trusting your life to God's hand does not mean that you will not experience hardship. But when you are with God, the Spirit fills you with His joy by giving you the mind to make the right decisions. The Spirit stays by you when hardship strikes and supports you so that you will survive its effects.

Notably, death in the name of Jesus Christ is a credible means to survive the problems of this world if the situation comes to that. His joy and security are not the same as the world could give, and His delightful will endures forever. Jesus said to the Samaritan woman,

Whoever drinks from the water that I give shall never thirst again because my water will become in whoever drinks it a fountain of water springing up into everlasting life.[61]

God's Need over Yours

The concept of balancing your life with faithful obedience means to let God's need rule over your need. Obedience to God implies not holding back when it comes to taking care of that with which He is concerned. Inherently, the body may hunger for physical food and the soul for spiritual nourishment. A combination of both types of sustenance duly keeps a person alive. The soul needs spiritual nutrients to survive, and the body needs natural food. If the soul starves, nothing for the body can help it revive.

---

61   John 4:14; John 4:1–26 – Jesus and the Samaritan woman

Servants of God must always hope for the best, even in times of severe hardship.[62] He is the giver of the living water and the provider of true protection. Denying God access to any part of you denies Him access to your entire self. There is only one way to God—the law of God broken, which we break when we sin, connotes righteousness as all-embracing. True worship is holistic; we either worship with our entire selves or not at all. If we do not give ourselves completely to worship, a single bad habit can shatter dozens of good behaviors.

Shutting God out of one or more of your habits could be your main spiritual weakness. Bodily weakness, when not restricted, is often the basis for spiritual downfall. Sometimes we cling to habits that sink us spiritually. It's not as if we lack the willpower to say no to the habits; rather, we stubbornly insist on keeping them. While persistence serves faith, stubbornness is usually in self-interest.

The story of the ten plagues of Egypt, found in the book of Exodus, is a reminder that, while the Pharaoh hardened his heart against God, God also hardened the Pharaoh's heart to prove him wrong. When one sets himself against God, God's mercy results even in further hardening.[63] Stubbornness is like the sin of rebellion, but it involves more than being strong-headed. Scripture associates stubbornness with idolatry and witchcraft. With the Judges and

---

62   "The Lord is good; a stronghold in all times of uncertainty" (Nah. 1:7).

63   "Pharaoh said, 'Who is the Lord that I should obey Him and let Israel go? I do not know the Lord and I will not let Israel go'" (Exod. 5: 2). "'Go,' Pharaoh said to Moses and Aaron. 'Serve the Lord your God. Who are the ones that are going?' 'We will go,' Moses said, 'but with our young and old; with our sons and daughters, with our flocks and our herds. We will go for we must hold a feast to the Lord.' Pharaoh said, 'The Lord be with you—if I let you go, along with your women and children! Clearly you are bent on evil'" (Exod. 10:8ff).

Kings, the scripture shows all forms of worship as less rewarding unless they are performed with an attitude of love and obedience. Prophet Samuel asked King Saul,

Has the Lord great delight in burnt offerings and sacrifices as in obeying the voice of the Lord?[64]

What Samuel is saying is that the reason for obedience is more serious than obedience itself. The secret of one's mind is revealed when the motive for one's actions is known. Worship is a bond between a person and God that demonstrates agreement between the two. If a person is not truly devoted to loving God, his or her worship could be less rewarding. Absence of heart, willpower, and substance in worship is a psychological ploy; these elements dignify worship and make it complete.

According to Paul, offerings should be voluntary, proportionate to one's means, and systematic; the spirit of brotherly kindness is an indescribable gift.[65] The Lord tests our will by asking that we donate to His house, not because He depends on us but as a symbol that we trust in Him:

A gift opens the way for the giver, and ushers him into the presence of the great.[66]

We improve our lives and the lives of people through charity because God loves cheerful givers.[67] He said,

---

64   1 Sam 15:22; "To do what is right and just is more acceptable to the Lord than sacrifice" (Prov. 21:3).

65   2 Cor. 9:15

66   Prov. 18:16

67   2 Cor. 9:7

I am the Lord your God. I do not rebuke you for your sacrifices or for your burnt offerings, which are ever before me. I have no need of a bull from your stall or of goats from your pens, for every animal of the forest is mine. I know every bird in the mountains, and the creatures of the field are mine. If I were hungry, I would not tell you, for the world is mine, and all that is in it. Therefore, sacrifice thanks offerings to God, fulfill your vows to the Most High and call upon me in the day of trouble; I will deliver you and you will honor me.[68]

Another good way to let God's need rule over yours is to have a thankful heart. A thankful heart is an important element of delightful worship:

Thankful heart makes the face cheerful, but heartache crushes the spirit.[69]

By discerning what occupies your heart, you are separating yourself from thought and worry, which are capable of influencing your total health and well-being. What you feed your mind is as important as what you feed your body. Having a delightful life of worship requires you to constantly thank God for His mercies in a similar way that you pray for your daily needs. You are not required by any biblical standard to deposit in the Church treasury everything you own in order to show yourself as having given it all. Such giving is not what God requires. God requires you to surrender yourself and all you own to Him, using your heart. To surrender all means to set everything aside for His purposes—to contribute to the services of His kingdom whenever necessary. When you do so,

68   Ps. 50:8–15
69   Prov. 15:13

your stock will, in due time, replenish through many means, and His Spirit will always be the joy of your heart.

Take tithe as an example. God said,

> *Bring the whole tithe into the storehouse, that there may be food in my house. Test me in this, says the Lord Almighty, and see if I will not throw open the floodgates of heaven and pour out so much blessing that you may not have enough room for it.*[70]

According to the Book of Leviticus, 'a tithe of everything from the land, whether grain from the soil or fruit from the trees, belongs to God.'[71] However, collection of tithe in Church is blown out of proportion; to an exaggerated view of the intended outcome. The theocracy that brought about the concept of paying tithe appeared to have vanished. Paying tithe is booming chiefly because tithe involved money; every pastor wants his or her congregation to pay up. But, was tithe meant to serve the pastor's need, or the need of the people, or both? Modern Church leaderships would not have provided the serious attention that we give tithe in our Churches if tithe is a code for character modification and living a godly life. Both the origin and the true purpose of tithe were recorded in Numbers chapter 18, Deuteronomy 14: 22-29, and Deuteronomy 26: 12-14. The principle at work was to ensure the support of the house of God and His workers, the Levites who received no salaries from their work and had no allotment from the land; which means no inheritance of their own. Portions of tithe served the need of the Levites, the sick, deprived widows, the very poor people within the community, and strangers who stayed in the house of the Lord.[72] As a society ruled by God, the arrangement

---

70   Mal. 3:10
71   Lev. 27: 30
72   Deut. 14: 28 - 29

of paying tithe was divine. Life in theocracy[73] is lived under the terms of divine law; there was no other formal taxation within the governing system except the people's tithe. The concept of theocracy is bound up with the fundamental concern of the Covenant. The promise, 'I shall be your God and you shall be my people'[74] brought every Israelite face to face with the will of God. Taken together, the three passages about paying tithe suggest the following:

- The Levites, who served as priests in the house of the Lord were mediators. They helped in governing the people through the rule of God's law and were rewarded with the collected tithe. As priest among the people, the Levites had the duty of promoting faith and holiness through delightful worshipfulness of the one true God.
- Annually, a tenth of all Israelite produce was to be taken to the city of the central sanctuary for distribution to the Levites.
- At an initial festival, all Israelites ate part of the tithe. The rest, which would be by far the major part of it, belongs to the Levites.
- Every third year the tithe was gathered in the towns and stored for distribution to the Levites and the less fortunate.

---

73   A theocracy is a society ruled by God. Yahweh was king in Israel; He was the commander of all legislative and judicial power. (Deut. 33: 5). The people were His army and their wars were Yahweh's wars. (Ex. 7: 4; Num. 21: 14).

74   Lev. 26: 12; "You have declared this day that the Lord is your God and that you will walk in His way, that you will keep His decrees, commands and laws; and that you will obey Him. And the Lord has declared this day that you are His people, His treasured possession as He promised, and that you are to keep all His commands." (Deut. 26: 17 – 18.)

The New Testament guide about Church donations indicates no principle for tithing, except to say that everything we own belongs to God. He gave all of our possessions to us. The Spirit wheel that has driven delightful worship since the beginning of biblical time has always placed God first. In 1 Kings, Elijah saved a Zarephath woman and her son from starvation as a result of the woman's obedience and faithfulness in giving. During the reign of King Ahab in Samaria, Prophet Elijah commanded the heavens to hold back its waters in order to prove that God is supreme in all ages.

King Ahab and his wife, Jezebel led astray the people of Israel, and they worshipped Baal. Elijah said to King Ahab,

As the Lord, the God of Israel lives, and whom I serve, there will be neither dew nor rain in the next few years except by my word.[75]

Elijah's word was quickly followed by a severe draught throughout the land, which caused the brooks to dry up.

Then the Lord said to Elijah,

Go at once to Zarephath of Sidon and stay there. I have commanded a widow in that place to supply you with food.[76]

Elijah met the widow at the town's gate while she gathered sticks, and he asked her for water to drink and a piece of bread to eat. The widow replied,

As surely as the Lord lives, I do not have any bread, but only a handful of flour in a jar and a little oil in a jug. I am gathering

---

75   1 Kings 17:1
76   1 Kings 17:9

a few sticks to take home and make a meal for myself and my son that we may eat and die.[77]

Elijah said to the widow:

Don't be afraid, go home and do as you have said. But, first make a small cake of bread for me from what you have and bring it to me; and afterwards make some for yourself and your son.[78]

Elijah's request implied a provision that the widow trust in God unfailingly. The widow overcame her fear and agreed to Elijah's request, relying on her faith. She served the need of the man of God, even though she knew that death could be next for her and her son. In faithfulness to His word, God miraculously provided for the widow and her son, and they survived the famine.[79]

The story of the Zeraphath widow is one particular reference that may not represent what will happen in our various situations of need; however, the message—that faithful obedience is a basic necessity of delightful worship—is clear. The Lord will always have compassion for His people and provide relief in difficult moments:

The sacrifices of the Lord are broken spirit; a broken and contrite heart, He does not despise.[80]

We can please God in whatever we do if our heart reconciles toward Him.

---

77   1 Kings 17:12

78   1 Kings 17:13

79   "'For thus,' says the Lord, God of Israel, 'The bin of flour shall not be used up nor shall the jar of oil be run dry until the day the Lord send rain on the earth.'" (1Kings 17: 14)

80   Ps. 51:17

Who Am I to My God?

Some people enjoy huddling; they make friends easily with strangers, and they are always surrounded by friends. Others do not like to huddle as much; they have fewer friends, and they feel uncomfortable talking with people they hardly know. These are some of the qualities that define our personalities, which relate to the way we serve God.

We are created equal and connected to each other, but we are each unique. Our different qualities enable us to produce different results. By possessing different talents, we are each the same people of God but in our own way. Besides talent, some people have opportunities in life that others do not have.

Nevertheless, God has made all great purpose in all that He made. You ought to be thankful for the person you are; this is not to say that you must be proud of your weakness and handicap. Be thankful because, in Christ, is the opportunity to develop the good in you and use the good to shape your entire personality.

Each person has a moral obligation to perform in accordance with his or her ability and to respect his or her limit. Many people are rarely satisfied with what goes on around them. They are never at rest. Striving to go beyond their natural gauge, they overstress themselves with too many works and become worried and depressed by the very means that should produce life's happiness. Such are people who take all the work upon themselves, rarely accepting that someone else could, in some way, be a better lead. Thus, these people deny their associates the joy of exercising *their* talents.

Jethro, Moses' father-in-law, said to Moses,

What you are doing is not good. You and these people will only wear yourselves out. The work is too heavy for you; you cannot handle it alone.[81]

---

81   Ex. 18:17–18

Moses failed to recognize the fault, so Jethro pointed it out. It is unnatural to be a jack-of-all-trades and the master of all. Moses did not have the energy to meet every need along the desert walk, but together with the appointed helpers, he accomplished most of what was required of him as the leader.

Members of Christ's community are likewise capable of distinguishing fruits, and regardless of how talented you may be, you cannot do it all alone. God can manifest His work through any one, but He does not give the entire ability to one person. God chose Moses to lead the Israelites out of Egypt, but this did not mean that Moses should preside over all minor details. Moses understood his father-in-law; he divided the necessary tasks among other talented Israelites.

In another situation, John the Baptist was asked to explain himself—to answer whether he was the Christ. John replied,

I am not the Christ.[82]
I am the voice of one calling in the desert, "Make straight the way for the Lord."[83]

To put John's answer in perspective, we need to value ourselves by appreciating the limits of our abilities, whatever those limitations and abilities are. Obeying the commandment of humility naturally prevents long-windedness.

Our worshipful relationship with Jesus Christ prepares us to know God better so that we can meet Him face-to-face hereafter. It is enough that every Christian satisfies the plan. God's struggle involves reclaiming humanity's devotion by reversing the effect of

---

82   John 1:20
83   John 1:23; "I baptize with water, but among you is one you do not know. He is the one who comes after me, the thongs of whose sandals I am not worthy to untie" (John 1:26–27).

negative forces that torment humanity. Despite your absorption in your own inner life, God provides you the strength to do exactly what He asks of you.

We live for God's kingdom in a similar way that John the Baptist was sent to prepare the people to recognize the Messiah[84] at His coming. Those who take approaches other than sincere worship oppose God's mission, just as the Pharisees did in the time of John's ministry. Strict and prophetic, John's concept of God's kingdom was not popular. The Pharisees and a majority of their followers expected the coming of the Lord to mean happiness for all, and they based their hope on a radical version of political liberation. John proclaimed that the kingdom would be ruled by righteousness and inherited by those who exhibited righteousness through the way they lived. The Pharisees did not appreciate John's message; they missed the point and insisted to have the proof of John's authority. By the same attitude, they failed to appreciate the Messiah.

Ironically, the Pharisees strongly believed in the prophets and were committed to daily observance of the law. But there was no limit to their religious pride. In light of John's witness, we see that his limitation was no hindrance but a key to his success. Talent is less important than how well one uses it to carry out God's purpose. We are rewarded more when we appreciate the ability we have by exercising it correctly.[85]

It is natural that human beings compete with each other in virtually every way. But the twenty-first century mind is explicitly competitive and values superficiality more than realness. Following the status quo, people consciously overstep the bounds of life by desiring to be something that they are not. They embrace superficial trends

---

84   In Hebrew, the word *Messiah* means the same thing as *Christ*, based on a Greek word, *Christos*. Both words biblically mean "the Anointed One," especially a king anointed for the task of fulfilling God's purpose.

85   Matt. 25:14–30 – the parable of the talents

to enhance their desired appearance. Romance with the unnatural constitutes desire for vanity, which steals joy in many people by pulling them out of themselves. The result is self-destructive, and such vanity promotes envy and moral chaos in our society.

Envy is armed with limitations that could extinguish anointing. When one is under the influence of envy, he or she is not concerned with reality, and enormous stress results from impressing people in unnatural ways.

Commending the potential that the Church has, the apostle Paul appreciated that we are not like the rest of the world:

We have different gifts, according to the grace given us. If any man's gift is prophesying let him use it in proportion to his faith. If it is serving let him serve. If it is teaching let him teach. If it is encouraging let him encourage. If it is contributing to the needs of others let him give generously. If it is leadership let him govern diligently. If it is showing mercy let him do it cheerfully.[86]

The gift of the Holy Spirit differs in nature, power, and effectiveness, according to His graciousness and wisdom.

The desire for superficial trends is circular; the net result is solely material success. You should not base your personal importance upon *what* you are and could be but on *who* you are. All of what you are can change in time, but your person is ever the same.

When Job's friends scorned his sad condition, he replied,

Doubtless you are the people, and wisdom will die with you! But I have a mind as well as you; certainly I am not inferior to you.[87]

---

86   Rom. 12:6–8
87   Job 12:1–3

Self-acceptance has the ability to safeguard against bias; if you have relaxed confidence, you can take on any of life's situations with whatever talent God provided you. If you cannot speak in tongues, you are not less gifted than those who can. Speaking in tongues serves no spiritual benefit to a Church with no one to give the interpretation.

For this reason anyone who speaks in a tongue should pray that he may interpret what he says."[88]

If you are an usher in your Church, your duty does not make you less important than the person who preaches the message. Neither usher nor preacher can render each other's services at the same time. The gift of the Spirit is evident by both a particular service and by the fruit that it prompts. Those who are apportioned different gifts serve the same Spirit. The criterion of authenticity is the common denominator—not of an elite group but of all believers. We need each other's help to move on. The preacher ought to be modest in giving the message and the usher in positioning the congregation to have a good service.

Self-acceptance motivates servants of God to maximize the use of their spiritual gift. The people you serve will appreciate you and take pride in your calling if your conduct is ethical, which includes appreciating both yourself and your limitations. Your good conduct will help your spiritual growth in similar way that your services help the people to grow in things of God.

The struggle is whether you can find yourself worthy of your calling. As you serve, do not worry about things that are not viable. Advance yourself with things that you have the opportunity to do better. Do not ask the Lord for a task identical to your strength but ask for strength identical to your task. The spirit that leads people

---

88   1 Cor. 14:13

away from their uniqueness is responsible for a cosmetic type of worship that engulfs our generation. Cosmetic worship indicates the visual rendering of "whitewashed grave"[89] by which Jesus describe the Pharisees and teachers of the law as no good. Those words of Jesus constituted bitter denunciation. Jesus never talked that way to common people. Jesus was the most genuinely religious man who ever lived, but His soul deeply despised religious pretence.

Worship as a performing art is like washing a cup only on the outside. For many Christians, confessing Jesus Christ as Lord is less desirable, that worship is for show. False adoration results from false piety and lack of true commitment to Christian doctrine. This fundamental crisis locks away a jealous and unrepentant heart. An unrepentant, jealous heart has a wicked way of comparing itself with others and a cruel way of admiring the things that other people have.

Against these avenues of hatred, the preacher said,

Anger is cruel and fury overwhelmingly, but who can stand before jealousy?[90]

Such jealousy as hatred shows no mercy when it takes revenge; its cruelty has brought about the downfall of many prophets and kings. A jealous person demonstrates no hope of getting blessings from God; those who are jealous carry within themselves the feeling that their needs will not be met and, thus, doubt their ability to succeed. In this way, jealousy is an attack on one's self and can hinder material and spiritual progress.

---

89   "Woe to you, teachers of the law and Pharisees, you hypocrites! You are like whitewashed tombs, which look beautiful on the outside but on the inside, are full of dead men's bones and everything unclean. In the same way, on the outside you appear to people as righteous but on the inside you are full of hypocrisy and wickedness" (Matt. 23:27–28).

90   Prov. 27:4

Jealousy ruined Cain by blocking the good sense that would enable him to worship God the righteous way.

We do not dare to classify or compare ourselves with some who commend themselves when they measure themselves by themselves and compare themselves with themselves, for they are not wise. We, however, will not boast beyond proper limits, but will confine our boasting to the field God has assigned to us, a field that reaches even to you.[91]

Paul indicates that works of faith are not based on any enticing wisdom of humanity; he urges your faith to stand, like the Holy Spirit, in the power of God. Those who uphold righteousness do not apologize for their experience of God's goodness.

It is the Lord who gives you power to prosper, and so confirms His covenant, which He swore to your fathers, as it is this day.[92]

Christians should not be indifferent to their limitations; nor should they contribute to their fellow servants' distress. A righteous poor is worth more honor than all of the riches of the wicked.[93]

The Law Made Manifest
We must qualify creation in light of pleasing God and according to whatever serves the well-being of the created universe. A life of delightful worship draws a balance between the present and the future in expectation of what the book of Revelation calls a

---

91   2 Cor. 10:12–13
92   Deut. 8:18; prosperity in the Lord does not necessarily mean money and material wealth; prosperity implies also spiritual progress and good health.
93   Prov. 28:6

new heaven and a new earth. The book of Revelation denotes the revolutionizing worship as inevitable by pointing ahead to yet another newness to be, which completes the human circle. The importance of the newness is the ongoing sanctification, or rather, revival by the Holy Spirit. We grow healthy in spirit by being qualified in holiness.

We ought to give thanks to God for creating us to be free and to have a purpose. The universe is indebted to God and fully dependent on Him for its origin and continuity. Life is a gift of love; and living depends on God and no one else. We must perceive all things according to their connection to the totality of creation, of which humanity is both a factor and a unique participant. The mutual connection indicates God as the center; both the universe and the rule of His law reveal him.

Our conscience bears witness to the truth in the same way that our thought accuses us of any wrongdoing. If your heart does not condemn you, you have confidence before God;[94] and if your conscience does not accuse you of any wrongdoing, you have the right standing before God. God's law was set in every heart, even before the law came down to Moses on tablets of stone.[95] Even though evidence of moral law appears in every culture, people insist on breaking those laws through making wrong decisions. The law God gave Moses and our consciences are not completely equivalent in purpose, but together they demand reverence to God. The law on tablets of stone[96] is objective, and conscience is subjective. Next to the law is the Holy Spirit who testifies to the use of conscience for justice. According to Jesus Christ before He ascended into heaven,

94   1 John 3:21
95   Exod. 19–20; Moses received the Ten Commandments on Mt. Sinai.
96   Exod. 20 – The Ten Commandments

Unless I go, the Counselor will not come; but if I go, I will send Him to you. When He comes, He will convict the world of guilt in regard to sin and righteousness and judgment. In regard to sin, because men do not believe in me; in regard to righteousness, because I am going to the Father, where you can see me no longer; and in regard to judgment, because the prince of this world now stands condemned.[97]

Since the creation, the Holy Spirit has been the executive arm of God on Earth, working to bring humanity back to the center. The Spirit of God has made us; the pattern is consistent in that He works to make us desirable to God.[98]

The Holy Spirit is greater than your conscience; thus, the first step toward healing your soul is to admit that you fit the human profile. The second step is to live in the best way possible by following ethical standards. Conscience is the Spirit's voice; it should not be confused with emotion or carnal thought. Emotions are no bad omen per se; their expression constitutes part of human nature. Danger arises when one exercise emotion through carnal mind.

As our minds are imperfect, they are corruptible and capable of many corrupt feelings. When we don't keep our minds right and control our feelings, the effect on our judgment could become a big spiritual hindrance. Spiritual maturity is not possible unless one learns to live beyond his or her corrupt feeling. Corrupt emotion is responsible for irrational decisions and bad behaviors, which are the results of the mind's corruptibility. If you allow wrong thought to override your good resolve, crisis is inevitable. One cannot intellectually process the things of God without involving the mind; so wisdom is required.

---

97   John 16:7–11
98   Job 33:4

The carnal mind is deceitful[99] and can create damage in the rest of the body. No one can live a successful Christian life while living a life ruled by emotion. Quite unlike conscience, we cannot rely on emotion for good judgment. You need either the law or conscience or both to discipline your thoughts and feelings.

The apostle Paul said that everyone is capable of doing things instinctively according to God's law. We obey God instinctively because of our consciences. The instinct responsible for good judgment is true human nature. Many people, especially unbelievers, ignore the course of true goodness; thereby, they do not naturally glorify God, even though conscience can sometimes force its way and make its presence known in their actions.

> *Since what may be known about God is plain to them, because God has made it plain to them. For since the creation of the world God's invisible qualities—His eternal power and divine nature—have been clearly seen, being understood from what has been made so that men are without excuse. For although they knew God, they neither glorified Him as God or give thanks to Him, but their thinking became futile and their foolish hearts were darkened. Although they claimed to be wise, they become fools."*[100]

All people are accountable to God for judgment according to the revelation that each person has. Those who possess the law on tablets of stone will be judged by the standard set forth by those standards, and those who don't will be judged according to their

---

99   "The heart is deceitful above all things and beyond cure. Who can understand it? The Lord searches the heart and examines the mind, to reward a man according to his conduct, according to what his deeds deserve" (Jer. 17:9–10).

100   Rom. 1:19–22

use of conscience.[101] If people are condemned on God's day, their condemnation will not be for the things they did not know about the divine mind-set but for what they did with what they knew.

God does not favor those who substitute the truth with anything else:

Since they did not think it worthwhile to retain the knowledge of God, God gave them over to a depraved mind; to do what ought not to be done.[102]

As the wicked reshuffle the truth to mean whatever supports their self-centered lifestyle, rebellion makes them slave to sin. There is no worse slavery than slavery to sin. Bad worship is the result of unfaithful servants twisting the truth for selfish gain while not engaging their consciences or considering the rule of God's law.

Again, conscience is the sense that separates right and wrong; it is the inner awareness of moral goodness and blameworthiness of one's own conduct, character, and intention. Conscience obligates one to do and to be that which is recognized as good. With conscience, everyone has an inner eye that sees God, which compels everyone to follow the ethical law.

Ethical law is consistent with conscience; together they promote delightful worship. No instinct guides civic law; one must have knowledge of an existing civic law in order to contemplate compliance. But conscience is instinctively unconditional; it is an efficient gateway to universal goodness. You must suppress your conscience to swerve toward iniquity.

Jesus developed the idea of the Holy Spirit as a personality and sent Him to support conscience in guiding us against wrongdoing.

---

101   Rom. 2:12
102   Rom. 1:28

Even so, we have choice and stubbornness prevails. It is, therefore, doubtful that any of the excuses for not worshipping God the proper way will ever be justifiable.

God has shown Himself to be the master evangelist, even before any human involvement in missionary work. It is common knowledge to believers that the law is entirely divine—a true reference to daily devotion, the code of conduct, and the authority to spread the Gospel. But we ought to keep in mind, especially when defending the truth, that God reveals Himself to every heart. We cannot do more than He has already done; we can but help the willing revive the truth in themselves. He who created the universe did not fail to reveal Himself in the very constitution of the created universe. Likewise, the Gospel is not telling the world something new about God, except that Jesus' attitude toward God is a model to regenerate.

God has no direct interest in punishing anyone; He set before us the good example and said,

I have shown you O man what is good; and what the Lord requires of you is to act justly, to love mercy and walk humbly with your God.[103]

God desires that we implement positive changes in our lives. He wants to see us live in a way that allows His transforming love to guide our ethical response to His mercies. It is impossible to follow God consistently without being part of His transforming love. People have tried to please God in other ways but without success. The choices that we make are crucial to our fate.

Accordingly, it is in our best interest to use our time on Earth ethically and wisely. The apostle Paul said,

---

103   Micah 6:8

See that you walk circumspectly, not as fools but as wise, making the most of every opportunity, because the days are evil. Therefore, do not be foolish but understand what the will of the Lord is.[104]

Life results in more complex hardships as people turn to perverseness. The suffering we endure when we avoid the work of darkness is huge. Nevertheless, children of God must lovingly continue to speak out the truth, exemplifying God's goodness in all works of life even when facing the challenges of the world in darkness.

---

104   Eph. 5:15–17

Chapter 2

⌒✒⌒

Bind to this World

B elief is practical in nature, especially when it applies to God. In worship, belief does not stand or act alone but complements love and discipleship. To believe in God is first to accept that He exists, which implies having knowledge of the truth, which brings salvation.

Mere belief does not gratify God; even demons believe that God exists.[105] A true and complete belief must exercise complete trust in God's word, the same way we must adhere completely to other elements of worship. Belief engulfs all of the elements to constitute working faith. Faith is the heart of worship, and faith without works is considered dead.[106] Our works of faith show the genuineness of our confession. We can work up human attitudes such as joyfulness, patience, and courage through effort, but faith erupts from our inner consciousness of God.

Faith is a priceless treasure in the workings of God's word; sadly nonbelievers in God hardly know the benefit. Seeking to better ourselves has unique meaning and provides more settling satisfaction

---

105   James 2:19
106   James 2:17

when we center our effort toward achieving the expected outcome on God. No one can seriously claim faith in God while barely accepting that God exists and refusing to see God as the almighty or honor His commandment. Anyone who believes while not incorporating these elements of faith has a futile belief.

A true belief commands obedience as an act of love. Without love, worship comes to nothing. Love is the perfection of human character and the most powerful tool of the Church. Its usefulness is more potent for building of the Church than any or all of the various manifestation of God's power:

> If I speak in the tongues of men and of angels, but have no love, I am only a resounding gong or a clanging cymbal. If I have the gift of prophecy and can fathom all mysteries and all knowledge, and if I have a faith that can move mountains, but have no love, I am nothing. If I give all I possess to the poor and surrender my body to the flames, but have no love, I gain nothing.[107]

Love unites all spiritual gifts and makes every gift more useful. Love is a commandment that embraces all commandments.

As the essence of God's nature, all people have the ability to love. Love descends from God's nature and implies that all of God's activities are loving activities. We must perceive true love within the Godhead; the demonstration of true love is evident in each person of the trinity. Those who join themselves to Jesus' sacrifice indicate their love for Him, and both the Father and the Holy Spirit love them. The rule of God's love is the only element of worship that indicates that keeping the law does not equal obedience. Outside love, it is possible to keep the law while being disobedient.

---

107   1 Cor. 13:1–3

Jesus disqualified the attitudes with which some Pharisees and teachers of the law approached worship. These leaders of the people may have kept the law, but practically, they failed in loving God and their neighbors. In view of such hypocrisy, which continues to result in faulty worship, it is not difficult to see how a whitewashed grave[108] may appear beautiful on the surface while hosting rotten things on the inside.

The World and Disobedience

The Bible points to violence as a major hallmark of human disobedience and warns about its dire consequences, consistently identifying violence with injustice and ruthless exercise of power.

So far, the flood[109] was God's severest judgment on violence, and He will reward righteousness again in eschatological judgment. In the Gospel according to Matthew, Jesus mentioned the flood as a historical fact and likens the time of His Second Coming to the days of Noah.[110] Leading up to the flood, the narrator explained,

The earth was corrupt in God's sight and was full of violence.[111]

While the flood cleansed the earth of a wicked generation, it did not cleanse human nature. The twenty-first is probably the most violent in history. Too frequent and sadly, the world grows in disobedience, increasingly lacking the true sense of love. Most common to our time is refined violence expressed in the so-called violence of principle—examples include the two sides of "the war on terrorism," moral blackmail, playing on imaginary fears,

---

108	Matt. 23:27
109	Gen. 6
110	Matt. 24:37–39
111	Gen. 6:11

brainwashing, social compulsion, dictatorial declaration, Internet censorship or withholding of information, and the denial of freedom of thought and expression. Also within law enforcement, violence is present in every corner of our society as a weapon of intimidation, persuasion, and protest.

The Gospel offers all people the opportunity of identical intellectual conviction as truthful means for peace and justice. The theme of loving your enemy and those who hate you is the foundation of Jesus' message asking for restraint and reconciliation.[112] According to Paul, revenge is strictly prohibited; believers are to leave room for God's wrath,

> *For it is written, "it is mine to revenge; I will repay" says the Lord.*[113]

By asking that we give food to our enemies when they hunger and drink when they thirst, Paul insists that mercy, which so graciously forgives, is the very thing that supplies us powerful and the irresistible urge to embrace goodness and transform our entire outlook on life. The cross personifies Jesus' victory over violence. His forgiving victory is the climax of the biblical story of violence.

Cain will always be remembered as the first to kill and arrogantly deny being his brother's keeper.[114] Cain cut off all of his fear of God and attended no more to God's ordinances, which led him to act wickedly against his brother. Since then, no one is free from works of hatred resulting from a bitter heart. As it is said, malice in the heart

---

112   Matt. 5:43–48

113   Rom 12:19–21

114   "Then the Lord said to Cain, 'Where is Abel your brother?' He said, 'I do not know. Am I my brother's keeper?' And the Lord said to Cain, 'What have done? The voice of your brother's blood cries out to me from the ground.'" (Gen. 4:9–10).

ends in murder by the hands. As the devil assumes more ground, violence slowly overshadows the world. It is not that the devil has absolute power or control; but worldly generations like ours set their hearts upon wicked things and are clever and industrious in exercising malice. Like Cain, our generation demonstrates hardness of heart by giving more concern to the consequences that we suffer rather than the gravity of our disobedience.

The Gospel holds to the truth—that we have no reason to be wicked, which should convince all of us to love the Lord our God with all our hearts and love our neighbors as ourselves.[115] We read in Leviticus,

> *Do not hate your brother in your heart. Rebuke your neighbor frankly so that you will not share in his guilt. Do not seek revenge or bear a grudge against one of your people, but love your neighbor as yourself.[116]*

It is common knowledge that most of the violence enacted in the name of religious belief has nothing to do with religion. People often invoke religious belief during conflicts that have social, economic, and political motivations. In some cases, the perpetrators of violence have no firsthand knowledge of the beliefs they pretend to join in order to be part of the conflict. The eagerness of wicked hearts, not any authority provided by religion, plays a major role in violence.

Our current generation perversely replaces moral guidance with empty riddles of idealism and carves images of idol as reality. When provocation, greed, and discontent embrace, the result is bitterness and, therefore, the continuing of violence. God will never accept the

---

115   Matt. 22:37–40
116   Lev. 19:17–18

world the way it is; His word predicts a flaming fire to destroy those who deliberately act against His command.[117]

Meanwhile everyone suffers the pain of our stiff-neckedness, which bars us from the peace of the Lord. The Lord said,

> *Do not be stiff-necked as your fathers were, submit to the Lord. Come to the sanctuary, which He has consecrated forever. Serve the Lord, your God, so that His fierce anger will turn away from you.*[118]

Like Cain, no one genuinely accepts the offer and no one is truly his brother's keeper. By being wicked, we make true love disappear. The weak and the strong are vulnerable to violence; and there is no end in sight to ambiguity. Give up the attitude that brings suffering to your doorstep.

> *If it is possible, as far as it depends on you, live in peace with everyone, and do not take revenge.*"[119]

Jesus Christ is like the offering of Abel; He models the ideal worshipful relationship with the Father. In humble obedience and by the righteousness bestowed on Him, His sprinkled blood speaks for reconciliation more than the blood of all departed saints. Jesus is the mediator of the New Covenant.[120] He is lifted up for every eye to see God through Him, but few behold Him.

---

117   "He will punish those who do not know and do not obey the Gospel of our Lord Jesus Christ. They will be punished with everlasting destruction and shut out from the presence of the Lord and from the glory of His power" (2 Thess. 1:8–9).

118   2 Chron. 30: 8

119   Rom. 12:18–19

120   "Therefore, see to it that you do not refuse Him who speaks" (Heb. 12:24–25).

Even within the congregation of Churches, the bitter thirst of hate is not quenched. Some Christians argue that Satan bears the full blame for the unrest in the world, but they forget that God blessed humanity above the curse of Satan:

> *So God created man in His own image; in the image of God He created him; male and female He created them. Then God bless them, and God said to them, "Be fruitful and multiply, fill the earth and subdue it, have dominion over the fish of the sea, over the birds of the air and over every living things that moves on the earth."[121] The fear and dread of you will fall upon all the beasts of the earth and all birds of the air, upon every creature that moves along the ground, and upon all the fish of the sea; they are given into your hands.[122]*

The commandment of God's blessing confirms also that marriage is the cornerstone of biblical standpoint on relationships between men and women. Man and woman are united to a unique social and community concept of God. Male and female He created them. This is God's special way of presenting family order—the basis for us to multiply and genuinely fill the earth. The authority of marriage love is given to humanity for humanity's welfare. In everything that God proposes, humanity stands on higher ground, above everything except God:

> *He that is in you is greater than he that is in the world.[123] Submit yourself, then, to God. Resist the devil and he will flee from you.[124]*

---

121   Gen. 1:27–28
122   Gen. 9:2
123   1 John 4:4
124   James 4:7

To listen to and obey Satan when we know that his demand goes against what God has commanded is reckless. The wickedness that we experience may frighten us, especially as things of this world try to overwhelm us. To make a difference, we must recognize the authority to overcome fear and use the authority for the intended purpose. Our problem settles in our state of mind. The wickedness of a generation brings a curse upon virtually everything that the generation does.

If we do not use our authority to overcome fear, our rebellion will trump tranquility. The world cannot find peace while humanity, the chief actor in world affairs, is exercising its authority incorrectly. When we do not engage against the evil forces that compel us but, rather, against our neighbors, the devil gains more liberty to act. He prospers while everyone suffers the consequences. We have the authority to defeat the devil. Jesus' life on Earth demonstrates the authority that humanity should walk in:

Our struggle is not against flesh and blood, but against the rulers, against principalities, against the powers of this dark world and against the spiritual forces of evil in the heavenly realms.[125]

To take a stand against the devil, we must put on the full armor of God, which is righteousness. Satan is the enemy. There is no doubt about his goal—he wants to sow confusion wherever possible. The all-knowing God has seen Satan's best efforts since the foundation of time. The continuing sovereignty of God, the King of Kings, constrains Satan's ability to corrupt. We read in Revelations,

They will make war against the Lamb, but the Lamb will overcome them because He is Lord of lords and King of

---

125   Eph. 6:12

kings and with Him will be His called, chosen, and faithful followers.[126]

It is your choice to live for the devil when you do not exercise correctly your authority against the things of evil, and it is your choice to live a rebellious lifestyle when you do not walk in the light of God's love. Satan is no threat to God's power of control. Whatever you may decide, your eternity from this life forward is at stake, not God's. God made us in a special way that enables us to take responsibility for our choices. As Reverend Kersten of the Dutch Reformed Church said, "There is a voluntary acting whereof the primary cause is God's decree and the secondary cause, the acting creature. This creature acts voluntarily; the secret decree does in no wise coerce him. God's decree is not the rule of the rational creature's actions but the rule of God's law. According to this law, the actions of man are deemed good or evil and neither the sovereignty nor the necessities of God's decree do at all remove the rational creature's freedom and responsibility."[127] We have the will to ignore the wrong attitude; and when we do not exercise the will correctly, it acts upon us like a curse. Satan may have certain influence over this life, but he certainly does not have absolute power or control. I urge the Church to do two things in this regard. First, the Church needs to regain the understanding of what it means to walk in the Spirit. Second, the Church's demand for righteousness must make a separation between the spiritual struggle and other social and political difficulties. Otherwise, many people may continue to be easily detoured. Jesus is, to the world, the Prince of Peace—the gift who saves.[128] Having been shown divine love that

---

126   Rev. 17:14

127   G. H. Kersten, *A Treatise of the Compendium*, 27.

128   John 3:16 "For God so loved the world that He gave His one and only begotten Son that whoever believes in Him shall not perish but have everlasting life."

is truly sufficient to save us, we have no justifiable reason whatsoever to embrace defiance.

The story of Cain and Abel is the first recorded example of man's inhumanity to man that is within the context of worship. Cain's sin is like the black spot on humanity's lens. Through that spot, every generation sees this life as the game of survival of the fittest. Humanity has engaged in a long history of warfare. Violent disobedience, such as invasion, murder, robbery, human sacrifice, prostitution, ethnic cleansing, and slavery modifies with each new generation. If might could always be right; love would be meaningless. Cain made himself arrogant against God by showing no remorse for killing his brother, Abel. He denounced his obligation to love[129] while he asked for God's protection.[130]

All people are God's children; yet the world is filled with people who admire killing. There is little doubt that humanity's intellectual strength brings more misery than it does good. We have the ability to reverse the status quo and serve the true purpose of goodness. Humankind must reverse its indifferent attitude and reflect the love of God toward his neighbor. Otherwise, many people will end losing the ongoing spiritual struggle, which they could have won. God gave us physical and intellectual strength for a good purpose—to love Him with all our heart and to subdue and inhabit the earth in an orderly way.

The desire to have all of our wants met, many of which are not really needs, has led to terrible abuse of strength. The result is an irresponsible waste of human lives and material resources, the

---

129   Lev. 19:18

130   "Cain said to the Lord, 'My punishment is greater than I can bear. Surely you have driven me out this day from the face of the ground; I shall be hidden from your face; I shall be a fugitive and a vagabond on the earth; and it will happen that anyone who finds me will kill me'" (Gen. 4:13–14).

exercise of arrogant pride by the perpetrators, and the suffering of unwarranted agony among the victims.

Considering worship through an examination of Cain's ordeal, one may wonder if it is a mistake that we worship God. It is Cain's heart of worship that caused his trouble. If Cain and Abel had not offered sacrifices to God, maybe Cain would not have killed his brother, and no curse would have befallen him.[131] This reasoning is adrift and does not reflect the true nature of the problem of evil. Those who consider worshipping God's through the lens of this reasoning easily find reason to blame God. Such people hold religion responsible for many troubles in the world, including their personal problem. Evil is an attack on our theological perception of God; it is not necessarily an attack on God Himself. God's steadfastness upholds justice, and the standard is unchanging. His judgment is timely and perfect. His grace endures. He is willing to give wrongdoers lengths of time to make a change of heart. It is our collective responsibility not to hate and seek revenge. We experience the implication through the damages hatred and revenge do to our society.

Many fanatics who use religion as a reason for conflict are like Cain; Cain suppressed his conscience and twisted the truth, which allowed the spirit of malice to occupy him. If wickedness had not overtaken the world, the people of the world would find room to act tenderly toward one another. We are like family; all persons who follow in Cain's footstep are ruining our chances of being truly happy. Cain was jealous of his brother's fortune. He hated his brother not because his brother had done wrong but because Abel had found favor from God through the righteousness of faith,

---

131   "So now you are cursed from the earth, which has opened its mouth to receive your brother's blood from your hand. When you till the ground, it shall no longer yield its strength to you. A fugitive and a vagabond you shall be on the earth" (Gen. 4:11–12).

For by faith Abel offered God a better sacrifice than Cain did. By faith he was commended as a righteous man, when God spoke well of his offerings. And by faith he still speaks, even though he is dead.[132]

Only a devoted heart can help people like Cain to imitate righteousness. One can learn righteousness by following a good example and by applying God's word to life's situation. Cain could have repeated his offering in a way that was acceptable to God, but he didn't. Cain could have rejoiced in his brother's fortune and, thereby, gained from God's blessing, but again, he didn't. By adopting good examples, we give support to the concern of moral value and help produce the fruits of ethical conduct.

Unfortunately, an attitude that allows one to humbly follow a good example is not popular among the children of men—it wasn't then and it isn't now. Living with a wicked heart is a big spiritual setback, and ignoring all divine signals calling for a change of attitude is an even bigger setback. Cain's real wrongdoing was not his unrighteous offering but that he refused to make amends, even after God reasoned with him concerning his attitude:

Then the Lord said to Cain, "Why are you angry? And why is your face downcast? If you do what is right, will you not be accepted? But if you do not do what is right, sin is crouching at your door, and it desires to have you, but you should rule over it."[133]

The truth confronts everyone in many moments of decision making. Your response to the truth is crucial to what comes next.

---

132   Heb. 11:4
133   Gen. 4:6–7

It is better to let the truth budge you toward making necessary amendments than to snub your sense of guilt. God's warning to Cain reinforced the biblical standpoint on the power of dominion, which we receive from God. Freedom is God's gift to humanity—we enjoy freedom of thought, freedom of conscience, and freedom of choice. The virtue of obeying God is in our nature; the inclination to do so will remain even though many people use their freedom to disobey God.

God was, then, available for Cain as He is for this dying generation. He encouraged Cain to withdraw his evil intention and put on the armor of righteousness. Equally, God is, in many ways, encouraging our generation to follow only the good and righteous path. As God reasoned with Cain to use his authority and rule over sin, the Holy Spirit works in the same authority and engages us to rule over evil with good.[134] The Holy Spirit motivates us to seek righteousness—that we maintain justice in order to live and not die.[135] The Holy Spirit's work is awakening; He works to help the world reconsider using malice to settle cases and engage wisdom in deciding where to spend eternity.

All people, like sheep have gone astray.[136] Many live like Cain, and they do not even believe in eternity. The challenge of helping lead these people back to the path of righteousness lingers, and the risk of losing many souls is obvious. The living should make amends, especially now that the opportunity to transform is real:

> *Now is the time to strengthen the hands, which hang down and feeble knees. Now is the time to make straight paths for our feet so that what is lame may not be dislocated, but rather be*

---

134   Rom. 12:21
135   Amos 5:14–15
136   Isa. 53:6

*healed. Now is the time to pursue peace with all people and in
holiness, without which no one shall see the Lord.*[137]

Each day is a day of salvation to the living, but the dead have
been deprived of the opportunity to amend. Worship is nothing
else but a means by which to transcend fear and make up for the
shortcomings in our daily lives by forming ourselves as part of God's
fold. It is, therefore, not helpful that God's truth is less popular
today, as the scripture predicts that the expectations of those in
need will not perish forever.[138] No one can attain God's standard
through the ordinary life on Earth. Yet exercising faith in God is
righteousness.[139] Jesus Christ has borne God's anger, which you
deserve. But that anger could fall on you on Judgment Day. God's
anger awaits those who reject the gracious sacrifice. Faith in Jesus
Christ is a genuine reliance on God's mercy; it is a heartfelt trust in
God's son, rather than in oneself, for salvation. It serves common
interest for us all to engage in worshipping God the right way. God
is not ruled by the will of men, therefore we cannot worship Him the
way we decide to do so. Convenient worship does not result in the
blessings that true worship brings; it has the danger of covering up
unholy practices among Church community. Convenient worship is
not justifiable by grace. Those who corrupt the Church should take
warning from what happened to fallen angels.

It is Christians' moral and pastoral obligation to help everyone
learn obedience. We must use the Bible, not science, not popular
worldview, and not gut feeling to judge the trustworthiness of our

---

137   Heb. 12:12–14
138   "How beautiful on the mountains are the feet of those who bring good
    news, who proclaim peace, who bring good tidings, who proclaim
    salvation, who say to Zion, 'Your God reigns'" (Isa. 52:7).
139   James 2:23

conduct. We must maintain the Gospel on its face value in order to show that the entire study of God is truly reliable.

Some Christians suffer emotional witchcraft; they believe that scientific truth and gut feelings are absolute. Their love of God easily evaporates, and their faith disappears like early morning mist when trouble strikes. Restraining oneself from giving into delusion and biased vision of the Bible requires applying the doctrine of faith correctly and diligently, not denying any aspect of God's law and Christianity's worth. It is unfair that some ministers speak of the Gospel in the name of Jesus Christ while they despise the doctrine, which ties the Christian faith to its root. We have among us Christian minds who accept His grace as a means to continue the life of sin.

Everything can be right[140] through the good use of wisdom and by following the truth. Nothing is made imperfect in the beginning; but when justice is driven backward, righteousness stands at a distance. It is not wrong to hate, and it is not wrong to be jealous. But hatred must be directed against the devil and all works of evil. Jealousy improves life when we only imitate the examples of good works. These are the kinds of hatred and jealousy that the Bible approves. Jealousy for holiness and hard work should transform into desire to be holy and hardworking. If your hatred of evil makes you avoid evildoing, then you have the right attitude. If you are a student, the right jealousy inspires you to study hard in order to be even more successful than the other students. Otherwise, rejoice in your neighbors' successes and be happy; your Father in Heaven will bless you for showing content in your neighbor's happiness. You cannot be adequately happy with the pace of your progress if you are not comfortable with the success your neighbor makes. No one should believe that if his or her falsehood enhances God's truthfulness and so increases His glory, he or she will not be condemned. Nor should

---

140   Eccles. 3:11

anyone believe that the sin that enables one to stay in touch with one's culture and the cultures around us is valuable. The apostle Paul said,

> *If our unrighteousness demonstrates the righteousness of God, what then we shall say concerning God? Could that mean that God is unjust in bringing His anger on us? Certainly not! If it were so, how could God judge the world?*[141]

No Unity without Obedience

It is unfortunate that the present-day pulpit generally diminishes the very motive that brought Jesus Christ to Earth. Jesus' time on Earth gave history a new beginning and a direction. His proclamation of divine providence is based on forgiveness and restoration to eternal life. The receiving of forgiveness presupposes the need to be forgiven, which brings up one of Jesus' most powerful appeals—the profound conviction of the reality of a future life in heaven. Our estate in heaven depends on our behavior on Earth, not necessarily on the receiving of divine forgiveness. Rather, it depends on an exercise among ourselves. A heart firmly fixed in heaven suggests a more careful relationship to the way we interact with others and things in this world. This world has an end, and heaven is forever. One should not approach this world with optimistic confidence in the things of this world, involving him or herself in the ways of life devised to secure maximum satisfaction.

By preaching a harmless Gospel of personal salvation to prevent destruction that will befall the system of this world, Jesus promised no limit to forgiveness, except for blasphemy against the Holy Spirit.[142] God forgives every sin of a repentant heart and requires

---

141   Rom. 3:5–6
142   Matt. 12:32; Mark 3:29

His worshippers to do the same. Forgiveness is one of the principal teachings of faith and a basic Christian attitude; yet many spiritual setbacks, like violence, result from severe shortage of the exercise. Jesus preached extensively on the need to have a forgiving heart as a means to obtaining mercy from God. He seems to imply that many people lose their souls because they are unwilling to forgive:

> *If your brother sins, rebuke him, and if he repents, forgive him. If he sin against you seven times a day and seven times comes back to you and says "I repent," forgive him.*[143]

We prove incapable of living up to the standards God has set because of our twisted minds; we often find determining when and how to forgive difficult. A personal way to deal with the difficulty is to ask God to increase your faith. An assignment from God can be seen as a gift. All believers desire faith to maintain the power to exercise godliness. In Matthew, chapter 6, Jesus states that it will be difficult to obtain mercy from God if we do not forgive:

> *For, if you forgive men when they sin against you, your heavenly Father will also forgive you. But, if you do not forgive men their sins, your Father will not forgive your sin.*[144]

To forgive is to give everyone, on a daily basis, a similar measure of mercy, which we receive from God. God's extensive mercy is the result of the redemptive blood of Jesus Christ, who believers must, through love, exemplify to all people. When you do not forgive, you deny our common ground as sinners and the need for God's care.

---

143   Luke 17:3–4
144   Matt. 6:14–15

God's mercy is not a direct result of our ability to forgive; the practice indicates that we truly understand what mercy implies. The apostle Paul said,

> *Get rid of all bitterness, rage, and anger, brawling and slander, along with every form of malice. Be kind and compassionate to one another, forgiving each other, just as in Christ, God forgives you.*[145]

Holiness abounds where love prompted by forgiveness abounds. Forgiving love is inseparable from holiness. As a key to worship, forgiveness has an obligation to give all concepts of peace a chance. We are sanctified by practicing forgiveness, which is how we prepare to go to heaven.

> *If any of you has a dispute with another, dare he take it before the ungodly for judgment instead of before the saints? Do you not know that the saints will judge the world? And if you are to judge the world, are you not competent to judge trivial cases? Do you not know that we will judge the angels? How much more the things of this life? Therefore, if you have disputes about such matters, appoint as judges even men of little account in the Church!*[146]

The basis for war and settling cases in civil court is often revenge. Unfortunately, vengeance helps nonbelievers of God to focus on the problems of the Church rather than on its purpose.

Church history is a dreadful manifestation of lack of forgiveness. Many people are resentful of the Church because of past events.

---

145   Eph. 4:31–32
146   1 Cor. 6:1–5

Centuries have passed since the Protestant Reformation, yet echoes of prejudice for and against the outcome still remain. The Church is noticeably divided and, thereby, does not fully appreciate the leading influence of the Holy Spirit.

The best result of our common history should manifest through the goals of the Holy Spirit, especially in spreading the Gospel. Without further looking backward, the Church of Christ must be reconciling and thankful for His abundant grace and protective love, which motivates missionary work. All Christians, despite Church denomination, are members of one family of God's people, where Jesus Christ is the high priest.

Like in every occasion where humans are involved, missionary work will occasionally result in some doctrinal disagreement on how to proceed. The apostles, Paul and Barnabas, had a few sharp disputes in this regard.[147] Nevertheless, the Church is forever one body. Our allegiance is to Christ and to the unity that He desires. His coming to Earth will be no less than an ingathering of the saints.

Paul acknowledged that the problem of division is carnally motivated when he asked the Church of Corinth,

Is Christ divided?[148]

Paul appealed to the Christian Church, saying,

"Agree with one another so that there be no divisions among you and that you be perfectly united in mind and thought.[149]

According to Jesus,

---

147   Acts 15
148   1 Cor. 1:13
149   1 Cor. 1:10

Every kingdom that divides against itself will be ruined; and every city or household divided among itself will not stand.[150]

The conventional borders tearing worshippers apart are not God's making. Rather, they are formed of people's opinions. People are taking Church segregation seriously, as if they are fighting war, but they forget that we are brothers and sisters of one source:

The body is a unit, though it is made up of many parts, and though all of its parts are many, they form one body. So it is with Christ. For, we are all baptized by one Spirit into one body, whether Jews or Greek, slave or free, and we were all given the one Spirit to drink.[151]

At one time, Jesus received a report from the disciple John concerning how the apostles had witnessed a stranger preaching and driving out demon in Jesus' name. They tried to stop him because he was not among the twelve. Jesus replied,

Do not stop him. No one who works a miracle in my name can soon afterward speak evil of me. For, whoever is not against us is on our side. I tell you the truth; anyone who gives you a cup of water in my name because you belong to Christ will certainly not lose his reward.[152]

Jesus clearly forbids the tendency to split His mission. This is because motive is a crucial test to determine when true service is at work. There is no room for narrowness and exclusivity among the Church. We have a common obligation to triumph over sin and

---

150   Matt. 12:25
151   1 Cor. 12:12–13
152   Mark 9:39–41

the kingdom of darkness. Again, the apostle James addressed the motivation for division as rivalry and strife and lack of forgiveness:

What causes fights and quarrels among you? Don't they come from your desires that battle within you? You want something but you don't get it. You murder and covet, but you cannot have what you want. You quarrel and fight. You do not have because you did not ask God. When you ask, you do not receive, because you ask with wrong motives, that you may spend what you get on your pleasures.[153]

Lack of forgiveness is indeed a serious setback. James's description of corrupt worship explains what happens when covetous desire living in unfaithful worshippers is sufficiently frustrated. Those who love pleasurable life more than they love God are problematic to devoted worshippers, as they are unfaithful to God.[154]

We should not base worship on societal norms but on God's word. That which is the norm is not always right. An instinct can instantly change a norm, but God's word is truthfully unchanging and eternally reliable. Worship based on human condition, like norms, does not facilitate forgiveness; those who follow only what is considered normal fall to the temptation of using the Church against its purpose. We must not forget that trials of various kinds are necessary in order for us to form godly character, as practicing

---

153   James 4:1–3

154   1Kings 21:1–16; King Ahab murdered Naboth the Jezreelite to take over Naboth's vineyard located close to his palace. Naboth had refused to lease his land to the king; it was his father's inheritance from the Lord. By Mosaic Law, ancestral heritage must remain in the family. Ahab's desire to have the vineyard was an open contempt against God's law. The property could neither be leased nor sold. Yet to fulfill the desire of the king, the king's wife, Jezebel, orchestrated a plot to kill Naboth. Naboth was wrongly accused of blasphemy and stoned to death.

forgiveness transforms into His likeness. Exercising mercy is an aspect of holiness that enables us to live in God's presence. Sin of the body affects spiritual well-being because body and soul are related in this life. It is not only the body but also the soul that will eventually suffer the final consequence of sin.[155]

Adulteration by Generations of the Flood

The flood[156] swept off the generation of Noah to form an end to its multiple sins. The people worshipped God with lust, and God call them the generation of idol worshippers. God saved Noah and his family to reward their sincerity.[157] The generations after Noah did not duly commit to doing things according to God's will; they lived in abundant sin.

The story of the tower of Babel is the mark of their disbelief of God's word

Never to cut off life again by waters of a flood; and never to let a flood destroy the earth again.[158]

The people raised a plan to build the city of Babel and a tower up to the heavens so as to reach God's dwelling whenever another flood or any form of disaster threatened the earth. Whatever that meant, the narrator was not concerned as to whether the people would

---

155   Matt. 10:28

156   "Then the Lord saw that the wickedness of man was great in the
        earth; and that every intent of the thoughts of his heart was only evil
        continually. And the Lord was sorry that He had made man on the
        earth. So the Lord said, "I will destroy man whom I have created from
        the face of the earth, man and beast, creeping thing, and birds of the
        air, for I am sorry that I have made them'" (Gen. 6:5–7).

157   "Noah was a just man, perfect in his generation" (Gen. 6:9).

158   Gen. 9:11

accomplish the task but with showing disapproval of humanity's disloyalty to God. God said,

Go, be fruitful and multiply; fill the earth and subdue it.[159]

But the children of men said to one another,

Come let us build ourselves a city, and a tower whose top is in the heavens; let us make a name for ourselves, lest we be scattered abroad over the face of the whole Earth.[160]

The people were biologically fruitful, but they exercised unfaithfulness by establishing the city of Babel and a monument to their own glory and greatness. The attitude did not please God; of course partial obedience is no obedience. The confusion of tongue that followed, along with the many difficulties that came with it were part of the consequence of disobeying God.[161]

Attitudes similar to those that motivated the children of men to build the tower of Babel motivates those who attempt to clone humans, make relaxing expeditions to the moon possible, and launch spacecrafts from Earth to other planets. All these endeavors gear toward celebrating the glory of man above the supremacy of God. Despite the benefit of these efforts to science, the problem is

---

159   Gen. 1:28

160   Gen. 11:4

161   "But the Lord came down to see the city and the tower, which the sons of men had built. And the Lord said, 'Indeed the people are one and they all have one language and this is what they began to do; now nothing that they propose to do will be withheld from them. Come let us go down and there confuse their language that they may not understand one another's speech.' So the Lord scattered them abroad from there over the face of all the earth, and they ceased building the city" (Gen. 11:5–8).

the spirit of man. The old spirit of rebellion, the worship of man, and human pride is again in control.

For a second time, God's grace—His withholding of judgment—will not last forever. The battle of Armageddon is a serious prediction in the Bible, which foretells that humanity will destroy itself by the system and coalition that it builds to protect itself. Motive qualifies behavior, and everyone who neglects God receives repercussion for doing so. Disbelief is usually the mark of unwillingness to obey God. Some scientists presume themselves the most high, instead of glorying God with the knowledge they have. God gave us the know-how to practice scientific study, and He deserves credit for all of human intelligence.

The world separates from God because activities in the world do not abide by God's guidance. The desire to free ourselves from God is not about something better, and it is not about anything higher than God. The inclination is lust, which we choose over integrity. Favored by modern science, homosexuality is one particular practice that clearly implies violent reaction to God's nature. The approval of homosexual acts contradicts the presumed wisdom of this world in such likelihood that some people dare to bring the practice into the house of God.

One of the ways in which the Old Testament has expressed the conviction against homosexuality is by placing a death sentence on the act. Using the law, the New Testament gave a new code to reconciliation, which is grace. Jesus said,

Go, but sin no more.[162]

I am not concerned about dismissing any psychological justifications for unethical practices like homosexuality. God does

---

162   John 8:11

not contradict Himself. Those who engage in homosexual acts are, in the same way as other serious sinners, provoking God to anger. They live by lust instead of by the word of God. There is no revival outside discipline. The depth of the irrational nature of sin rests on the fact that hardened sinners know that their action deserves death, yet they go on sinning the same way and drag people down with them. Homosexuals rejoice in sin, and they approve those who imitate them.

Freedom is a good thing to enjoy, but freedom serves no useful purpose when it is a tool for self-destruction. The way some people exercise their God given freedom is suicidal; their lifestyles destroy the basic goodness that provides their freedom. God sets us free from the bondage of sin and allows us freedom of choice. We can both live by faith within the framework of law and grace and have everlasting life, or we can live in sin and die as its slave. The first option is made possible by God's righteousness; in this way, He justifies sinners by putting them right to Himself without compromising His absolutely pure moral character.

Human beings are equipped with common sense so that we can engage in making right judgments. In sin, we fail God and ourselves. Humanity's recklessness sets the wrong foundation for the future. Dependability on God is inevitable; imperfection cannot suddenly give birth to perfection. Hence, false belief breeds immorality. To use personal freedom to dismiss God's leadership is like dismissing the very basic goodness on which humanity stands, allowing us to have part in divine grace. It is illusive to hope for grace while being deliberately disobedient.

Let us not consume all our energy arguing about God's word; let us start applying it and let it loose in the world. Let us seek answers through diligent Bible study and meditation. Let's heed the Bible's summons, grasp its message, follow its directions, and trust its power. Let those acquainted with His truth lift up their voices without fear and prejudice and make His truth known.

Law and Grace

Grace is not justifiable without the law, and the law cannot make one perfect without grace. Jesus' death on the cross is God's amazing solution to humanity's problem. The Gospel does not abolish God's moral plan but forms part of the entire plan, which is redemption. Jesus Christ, in obedience to the law, died and paid the penalty for our breaking of the law. His action makes God's moral standard eternally valid.

In order to have spiritual life, we need both the law and His grace. The essence of the law mandates that we should be godlike, but the law alone is not enough to earn salvation. The law is not meant to give a list of commandments for every occasion but to identify sin and bring people back to God. The mistake of the Pharisees was thinking that they could get to God by simply following the law. In their misguided opinions, the law was simply a system of earning righteousness in one's own strength. There is no way that anyone could fulfill the law in its entirety given the nature Adam left us:

No one will be declared righteous in His sight by observing the law; rather, through the law we become conscious of sin."[163]

The modern Christian lives in disobedience and hope that God's grace will be sufficient to ensure his or her salvation.

Why did God give us the law if we can so sufficiently earn grace? And what is grace to the law? The law is not only a standard on how to behave; it also provides access to God. The moral code revealed in the law serves to guide our actions by holding to God's standards. According to the apostle Paul, the law is never intended to save anyone. Rather, like a mirror, it shows us what and where we have done things wrongly. The law does not bring about redemption; it

---

163   Rom. 3:20

points to the need for redemption. The law is limited; it cannot make us right unless something is done about our nature; this is what Jesus Christ did. The law made nothing perfect, so Jesus introduced a better hope, by which we draw nearer to God.[164]

The law of the spirit of life, through Jesus Christ, makes grace obtainable for all. The law is good and sacred, but it could neither provide the fullest ability to fulfill its demand nor the atonement necessary to redeem those who violate the demand. What the law could not do God did through Jesus Christ. Jesus is the offering for sin; this offering was made in the likeness of the flesh in order that the requirement of the law be fulfilled. With the law, we know the need for grace, and with grace, we appreciate the law.

The problem regarding the law is that it provokes sin by revealing that we have sin in us. Without the law, we wouldn't know what sin is. The law is the only reason God's demand for obedience is genuine. The law demands obedience as belief is to trust in God's grace. The new covenant implies that the problem of sin is resolved. Once and for all, Jesus took care of sin with the bestowed righteousness of God. In Him, you have the ability to get over your sin, retracing your footstep to join the path of righteousness.

Commitment to Christ is righteousness. Righteousness is, therefore, a matter of openness to God's grace. God know about your weaknesses before the law could point them out. Confession and works of righteousness help to forsake wrongdoing. The preacher says,

> *He who covers his sin will not prosper. But whoever confesses and forsakes his sin will have God's mercy.*[165]

---

164   Heb. 7:18–19
165   Prov. 28:13

With catechism, I learn that confession is the first step toward amendment, which indicates one's willingness to reconsider. According to the prophet, Jeremiah, it is through the Lord's mercies that we are not consumed, because His compassion fails not.[166] But unless one acknowledges his or her sin and sincerely confesses, the sin may continue to bring about an emotionally distressed life, filling one's life with groaning. The psalmist said,

> *When I kept silent, my bones wasted away through my groaning all day long. For day and night God's hand was heavy upon me; and my strength was sapped as in the heat of summer. Then I acknowledged my sin to Him and did not cover my iniquity. I said; "I will confess my transgressions to the Lord and He forgave the guilt of my sin." Therefore, let everyone who is godly pray to God while He may be found.*[167]

A commitment to faithfulness may be painful and difficult to maintain, but the exercise bring a reward that will serve you for a long time. God demonstrates His unfailing love by preserving the solemn promise never to destroy the world again by flood. He desires to save the world, but the world must first choose to be saved. Collective approval of God's salvation is unlikely, so Jesus made it individually possible. Salvation is, by all means, a personal choice. God's unfailing love implies that the success of a true Christian life is not that of the Christian but of God, who shines through him or her.

You may be weak, and sometimes I wish we were weaker. Faced with the forces of evil, we are often tempted to put on a show of Christian strength. But it is in our weakness that Christ's strength

---

166   Lam. 3:22

167   Ps. 32:3–6

is made perfect, and it is words of human weakness that the Holy Spirit endorses with His power. So it is when you acknowledge your weakness that you can be made strong. God sustains you; and you must allow His Spirit access to stream into your heart. Otherwise His influence may never be forced on you.

> *This is the same message that you heard from the beginning, to love our God by loving each other. Let us not be like Cain who belonged to the evil one and murdered his brother because his own actions were evil and his brother's were righteous.*[168]

---

168   1 John 3:11–12; "This is how we know what love is; Jesus Christ laid down His life for us and we ought to lay down our lives for our brothers. Let us not love with words alone but also actions and in truth" (John 3:16–18).

Chapter 3

Our Father

U nder the stress of physical and emotional suffering, Job said,

Who is the Almighty that we should serve Him? What would we gain by praying to Him?"[169]

Job's frustration is matter-of-fact. Faced with death and decay, Job did not give up hope on God, the redeemer. As a person in great need to have comfort, he spoke honestly to God about his feeling to let out his frustration.

But his deep grief limited his perspective of God and his finite understanding of life, which added to his protest that the wicked seem more prosperous than the righteous. Job referred to his integrity because he initially felt that God treated him like an enemy.

Why should the wicked live on, growing old and increasing in power? When I think about this, I am terrified; trembling seizes

---

my body. They see their children established around them; their offspring before their eyes. Their homes are safe and free from fear; the rod of God is not upon them. Their bulls never fail to breed; their cows calve and do not miscarry. They sent forth their children as a folk; their little ones dance about. They sing to the music of tambourine and harp; they make merry to the sound of the flute. They spend their years in prosperity and go down to the grave in peace. Yet, they say to the Lord, "Leave us alone! We have no desire to know your ways."[170]

The opinion is similar to David's concern in Psalm 73 over the same subject. David said,

But as for me, my feet had almost slipped; I had nearly lost my foothold. For, I envied the arrogant when I saw the prosperity of the wicked.[171]

Like Job, David lived the experience of life's threatening hardship, most of which his enemies plotted. Job and David's protests appealed for a hearing, which ironically challenged their oversimplified doctrine of justice. Their views seemed to echo the beliefs of God's faithful worshippers, who still question the justice in allowing the wicked to prosper while the righteous endure much hardship.

David looked upon the wicked as not caring about God's way. Yet he saw the wicked prosper in almost everything they did:

---

170   Job 21:6–14

171   Ps. 73:2–3; Psalm 73 is David's prayer, which Asaph the Levite recorded. 1 Chron. 15:16–19 and 2 Chron. 29:30 show Asaph as one of the three Levites appointed by their brothers as leaders of David's Levitical choirs. He is mentioned as seer to those who sang David's songs for the Lord's worship in the time of King Hezekiah. Collections associated to Asaph include Psalms 39, 42, 49, and 50.

They have no struggles; their bodies are healthy and strong. They are free from burdens common to man; they are not plagued by human ills. Therefore pride is their necklace; they clothe themselves with violence. From their callous hearts comes iniquity; the evil conceits of their minds know no limits. They scoff and speak with malice; in their arrogance they threaten oppression. Their mouths lay claim to heaven, and their tongues take possession of the earth. Therefore their people turn to them and drink up waters in abundance. They say, "How can God know? Does the Most High have knowledge?" This is what the wicked are like—always carefree, yet they increase in wealth.[172]

The wealth of the wicked may seem inviting when one considers it through unqualified imagination. Therefore, it is no surprise that some people of God may, under the stress of hardship desire to enjoy life like the wicked. When facing hardship, many people do not think about how suddenly the wicked may come to a shocking end. David acknowledged this mistake when he realized that justice will be served. He called himself

Senseless and arrogant; as stupid as a beast before the Lord.[173]

David said,

When I tried to understand all this, it was oppressive to me until I entered the sanctuary of God; then I understood their final destination.[174]

---

172   Ps. 73:4–12
173   Ps. 73:21–23
174   Ps. 73:16–17

The Holy Spirit helped David realize that his notion of the "prosperity of the wicked" was practically unreliable. His viewpoint did not reflect the true nature of God's justice. Like people who sometimes lose self-control as a result of life's bitterness, David was embittered by envy because of his grieving heart; he forgot that the Lord was always with him and held his hand.[175]

However, the idea of righteous suffering is one of the most common problems of the Old Testament believers. The people were often made to learn obedience through suffering.[176] In many practical ways, the temptation to imitate the prosperous ways of the wicked is still active and drags down many trustful people. There is little doubt that material progress by those who do virtually nothing to please the Lord is psychologically disturbing, especially now, as faithful people endure a very materialistic age.

Many people do not believe that true happiness is possible when desire is based only on God. As people have for all times, our generation wants to gain all of God's blessing without befriending God. We cry out for comfort, security, and relief; yet we fail to take the first step, which is to turn away from sin and open the channels to God. Those who prefer to enjoy the world in an ungodly manner fail to recognize that God is not against prosperity and happiness. God placed humanity on top to take charge of the earth. As moral creatures, humanity should adopt divine mind-set as its principle guide for good governance.

Unfortunately, the progress of our time is such that unfair judgment and greed are abundant. Everyone can, in fairness, gain from the mass wealth on Earth without being so sinful. But we have a sense of urgency that pushes us to seek wealth more than is

---

175   Ps 73:21–22
176   Jer. 12, Hab. 1, and Mal. 3:13–15

necessary to attain the ordinary happiness of life. The wealth of the wicked is a huge moral liability. Unclean riches may suddenly lose their value, but righteousness is valuable eternally.

Toward the end of his suffering, Job realized that God's way is perfect. He apologized for his wrong ideas and corrected his thought. Job said to the Lord,

> *I know that you can do all things; no plan of yours can be thwarted. Surely I spoke of things that I did not understand; things too wonderful for me to know.*[177]

From all practical perspective, greed leads to loss of spiritual direction. Our world consists of a people that need God's healing daily; they torture themselves being envious of other's lifestyles. Paul said,

> *Where sin is increased, grace increased all the more, so that, just as sin reigned in death, so also grace might reign through righteousness, to bring eternal life through Jesus Christ our Lord.*[178]

Paul admits human nature in life's unpredictability and implies that all people are incurable of the need of God.

With the current circumstance, believers who mature by experiencing God at work are likely to understand how every situation could eventually benefit those who trust in God. The trials of our time may, in the end, give potential for a great praise. Meanwhile, a wise person lives in view of what he or she knows as true about God, the world, and him or herself; a wise person does not accuse God of any wrongdoing but makes him or herself humble. We are

---

177   Job 42:2
178   Rom. 5:20–21

enabled to communicate our concerns freely to God because God's relationship is genuinely personal.

Prayer and Worship

Humanity is traditionally religious, and no matter the circumstance, people will always depend on the Supreme Being. The concept of God is inborn; no one can get rid of God. Believers who experience great trials have the potential to understand the secret power of prayer. Those who have not experienced great suffering may not appreciate God in so wondrous a way as those who mature under severe hardship. Paul said,

> *For this reason, I kneel before the Father from whom His whole family in heaven and on Earth derives its name.*[179]

Addressing the Father by His name grows the awareness of belief and, in reverence, expresses our deep emotional connection to Him. In other words, the ultimate reward of prayer is fellowship. Prayer in the Bible addresses the personal God. God exalts those who pray to Him and brings them to an honored nearness of His presence. As a key could open the door of a house and give someone the right of entry to the house, so does prayer lead to the presence of God. Through prayer, one can talk to God about everything. The Bible indicates that prayer is the heart of worship. Inseparable from spirituality, prayer commands all communication with God.

A Church assembly that is biblically and evangelically motivating matures through prayer. Accordingly, the assembly will give special attention to the life of prayer. Prayer is one of the oldest traditions of worship, which began in the line of Seth after Cain murdered his brother, Abel.

---

179   Eph. 3:14

At that time, men began to call on the name of the Lord.[180]

Prayer is particularly necessary where sin and cruelty is king. The reason to pray is to subdue rebellion and adopt the loyalty that God demands. Nothing will inspire the desire to pray except heartfelt need for God and gratitude for His works of redemption. The gift of prayer is powerful and compassionate; it is the will of God that makes prayer real, and only He answers prayer. God is able to do immeasurable things—more than we can ask—but we ought not be too determined to bring everything about prayer within the range of our limited understanding.

If only we persevere, committing to the practice of prayer and applying ourselves with enough patience, we could reach attainments that we do not ordinarily dream possible. Such an attitude presupposes that God's ultimate will is unchanging, but the way in which He chooses to realize His will may well depend on the petition of His children. The wise do not trust in oppression for riches; they do not rob in order to survive. Rather, they trust in the power of prayer through hard work. When riches increase, the wise do not set their hearts on those riches, owing to the fact that every of life's occasions is a subject for prayer.[181] David said,

God has spoken once, twice I have heard this: that power belongs to God. To Him also belongs mercy.[182]

---

180   Gen. 4:26

181   "If I have put my trust in gold or said to pure gold, 'You are my security,' if I have rejoiced over my great wealth, the fortune my hands had gained, if I have regarded the sun in its radiance or the moon moving in splendor, so that my heart was secretly enticed, and my hand offered them a kiss of homage, then these also would be sins to be judged, for I would have been unfaithful to God on high" (Job 31:24–28).

182   Ps. 62:11–12

God is not limited to any geographic location; everyone who prays will experience God's salvation. God can turn sea to wilderness and water spring to dry land. God can make a fruitful land barren for the sake of wickedness. He can make wilderness a water spring that the righteous may dwell peacefully on the land.[183] Devote yourself to prayer; asking for the right things takes wise discernment.[184]

Jesus prayed immensely and sustained Himself with prayer throughout the events that marked His ministry and crucifixion. If Jesus needed to pray, how much greater is the need of prayer to His followers. Knowing that prayer could influence our material and spiritual well-being, Jesus explained prayer in ways to encourage His followers to pray often. He taught about prayer not just in relation to meeting our material needs; essentially prayer links us to the kingdom of heaven. One who prays believes in God's saving power and providence.

Many Christians do not pray because they do not meditate on God's word. Biblical spirituality makes room for a special kind of silence used to prepare the mind for stages of prayer. Addressing the importance of prayer, God solemnly advised Joshua on the threshold of his leadership task to be prayerfully careful, to keep close the teachings of the law, and to meditate on the task day and night.[185] According to the Lord, Joshua's success and prosperity depended on meditation and prayer, as Joshua did all things according to the instructions of the Lord.

One can learn the exercise of prayer through meditation. Meditative Bible study leads the mind to prayer by saturating the mind in things of God. One cannot accomplish the effectiveness of prayer by formula but with relationship. God's relationship with leaders like Moses, Joshua, King David, and King Hezekiah enabled

---

183   Ps. 107:33–38
184   Matt. 7:7–12
185   Jos. 1:8

them to make intercession for the people, as these leaders believed that God was pleased through meditation and prayer. The belief prompted David to ask that his thoughts about God's word and songs of praise be acceptable as though they were prayer offerings brought to the altar.[186]

In Church community, corporate prayer serves the sanctity of the entire body of Christ, and personal prayer is for the sanctity of oneself. One can confidently encourage prayer, as to pray is to ensure God's nearness. He hears His people from everywhere while bearing the awareness that shapes the response of prayer. God's supreme power does not make prayer pointless.

Through prayer, believers are constantly drawn to the triune God; the Spirit of the Son joins them to the Father and affects in them a living union.

The Spirit, Himself, testifies with our spirit that we are indeed children of God.[187]

The Spirit's presence is what Jesus had in mind when He said to His disciples,

I will never leave you nor forsake you. Neither the Father forsakes His inheritance.[188]

By taking to heart God's nearness, a prayerful Christian may boldly say,

Jesus is my helper, therefore I fear no evil.[189]

---

186   Ps. 19:14
187   Rom. 8:16
188   John 14:17–18; Ps. 94:14
189   Heb. 13:5–6; Ps. 54:4

In Him we can become fearless by facing our fear.

Prayer is both an activity and a relationship, a gift and a task. God leads the initiative by revealing His desire, and we respond by expressing our innermost selves to Him. The habit of prayer can be exercised both corporately and individually. Jesus put considerable emphasis on secret prayer, but He does not rule out public prayer. We should never be ashamed to pray. A believer who accepts God's presence worries about nothing; through petition and testimony of faith, believers receive the answers to life's questions.

Despite the time it may take to attain desirable results from prayer, we should, at all times, consider, through faith that God's hand will take care of our need. David safeguarded his kingdom against his enemies by trusting in the Lord's nearness. He asked his counselors,

Is it not in the Lord that I put my trust, how dare you say to my soul, "Flee like a bird to the mountains?"[190]

Through many prayers, David testified his solemn trust in God; he believed that God was always on his side. God's omnipresence illuminates believers to trust and praise.

Those who look to Him are radiant; their faces are never covered with shame.[191]

It is important that your prayers constitute biblical speech. Exercising the word of God in prayer is part of the speech function of prayer. The nature of prayer includes thanksgiving, plea of mercy, and intercession. A combination of the variety is typical of the book

---

190   Ps. 11:1
191   Ps. 34:5

of Psalms. In a single collection, a psalm may contain prayers of a similar nature of prayers. Prayer is an effective way to solve problems. I appreciate the prayers in the book of Psalms— how God's attentiveness to those prayers makes worship an interesting thing to do.

My prayer brings God's attention nearer to my concern. God provides my way out when I am tempted. He foresees the outcome and provides the support that allows me to rise above each circumstance. I am familiar with the way problems are sometimes solved in ways that I cannot easily see. His divine intervention in the course of many struggles strengthens my hope for better days ahead in similar ways that praying accomplishes my dream for His love. What is doubtful is not whether God hears my prayer and adequately rewards me but how often I listen to God and adequately follow His guidelines. This is true of me, as it is also true of many Christians.

My frustration when it comes to prayer is not about things that constitute my real needs. God provides my daily bread, but I want to have everything that I desire. This is the difference between answered prayer and prayer we assume has gone unanswered. God does not let His children stumble about, looking for solutions to their problem. His word is always with His children and constitutes the solution to every problem. Cherish whatever you have and develop empathy to pray.

God's children ought to show contentment, knowing that God will sufficiently answer their needs. Otherwise, multiple petitions and objections could turn to selfishness when desires are not balanced with contentment.

I have learned the secret of being content in any and every situation; whether well fed or hungry, whether living in plenty or in want. I can do everything through Him who gives me strength.[192]

---

192   Phil. 4:12–13

One God: Too Many with Need

One of the biblical assertions about God is that He speaks. He reveals Himself and His will by interacting with people. We know who God is because He communicates Himself. He provides the framework for communicating the present and the future.

The Bible contains precisely the things that God wants humanity to know, in exactly the form in which He wants us to know them. The Bible is the platform of God's utterance and the one and only answer to humanity's quest for God. Everyone ought to love the Bible, read it regularly, and strive to live by its teaching. God expects us to respond to His goodness through ethical behavior and by communicating our desires to Him.

Many people are reluctant to talk to God; thereby, they deny themselves the chance to express their opinions to divine means. While some Christians are simply too lazy to pray, nonbelievers use excuses, such as the failures on Earth, to avoid prayer.

We are in a relationship, and praying reminds God about everything we feel as a result of personal situation and earthly circumstance. Your life is a gift from God, and you are challenged through the experiences of living to always reason with God on issues concerning both your experience and His requirement. There are days when the last thing one may wish to do is pray and rejoice in the Lord, especially when many situations are out of our hand. In downcast moments, you have the right to say that it hurts. Tell God how you feel in prayer, and He will console you and give you reasons to rejoice. Surely the Lord is your helper. He alone can sustain your desire. God said,

> *If ill befalls you or if anyone attacks you, it will not be by my doing, but whoever will attack you shall be made to fall for your sake.*[193]

---

193   Isa. 54:15

Even though you have personal concerns, the Bible reminds you to always intercede on behalf of the company of saints and the whole world. It is gainful to remind God in prayer about the problems of the world, particularly the problems of your immediate Christian environment. Otherwise, praise Him in all situations. Your petition may result in help to overcome certain conditions, if you pray often. By your supplication, God will distinctively stand up against the forces that fight you.

In days of trouble, David prayed,

Challenge O Lord with those who challenge with me; fight against those who fight against me. Take up your shield and buckler; arise and come to my aid. Brandish spear and javelin against those who pursue me. Say to my soul, "I am your salvation."[194]

Cruelty is a daily reality in many lives. Therefore, David's call for justice—a call I encourage you to repeat—is not a cover-up for personal vengeance. In circumstances of unjust treatment, the soul can be joyful again by turning to the Lord. However, your petition for justice does not make God responsible for your trouble. Your petition acknowledges that God is truly the source and the hope of your life. He has the obligation to protect you according to His wisdom.

Moreover, prayer will somehow focus you on the good things that God is doing in your life. It is easy to complain about life's circumstance, but the psalmist outlines plenty of reasons to praise God:

You forget not the benefits of He who forgives all your sins and heals all your diseases, He who redeems your life from

---

194   Ps. 35:1–3

destruction, who crowns you with loving-kindness and tender mercies, He who satisfies your desires with good things so that your youth is renewed like the eagle's.[195]

Psalm 103 teaches prayer as an opportunity to praise God first and thereafter request His divine intervention in your life and in the lives of people around you. The prayer of Psalm 103 is an act of faith that does not focus solely on God's future promise. The Psalm, like all ideal prayer, looks backward to acknowledge blessings gained.

Despite the difficulty in life's journey of faith, you can always count your blessings in God; otherwise your prayer of personal intercession will be self-centered and out of balance. A believer who emphasizes only the need to have a good self-esteem and positive image indicates preoccupation with him or herself; such a believer is ignorant of the word and works of God and selfishly proud. Your prayer should not always be about you. Sometimes prayer must include thanksgiving and the needs of other people. God's children receive the fullness of joy by asking for other peoples' needs and by giving thanks. The prayer of a faithful Christian can affect his or her neighbors in many wondrous ways.

We live in a challenging world wherein there is no doubt that wickedness dominate among its inhabitants. The consequence of human misbehavior is stunning. But as a believer, you are not left to your own resources while you cope with the problem. God delights in hearing you pray in the same way that the Holy Spirit delights in helping you step over the devil's stronghold. The Holy Spirit will rewrite your petition when you do not know the right word to pray:

---

195   Ps. 103:2–5; the Old Testament defines God as divine healer. The definition is based on the character of Yahweh as the great healer. In the Psalm, the dimension of healing referred to is specifically to include physical wholeness. God does not only forgive our sin, He also heals our diseases.

The Spirit Himself intercedes for all of us with groans that words cannot express.[196]

It is offensive to God when we fail to pray. As hope sustains us when we suffer, so does the Holy Spirit help us when we pray.[197] Otherwise, a mind that swings is not completely convinced that God's way is the best. God does not respond to prayer composed with doubt and critical attitude. The apostle James said,

Let him who asks, ask in faith, not doubt, because he who doubts is like a wave of the sea driven and tossed by the wind.[198]

We ought to address the Father in prayer through the Son and the Holy Spirit. The combination fulfills the purpose for which the Father sent the Son and the Holy Spirit. To some believers, Prayer is the charismatic breath of Christ. In some congregations, prayer is simply a testimony of one's faith, an expression of oneself to God. Despite different factions of the Christian faith holding slightly different approaches to prayer, the Gospel is clear in showing that Jesus Christ prayed to the Father in an unbroken communion and so should we.

We cannot pray to the Father without involving the Son and the Holy Spirit; it is in union with the Son and the Holy Spirit that we are children of the Father. The Holy Spirit reveals our

---

196   Rom. 8:26; "And He who searches our hearts knows the mind of the Spirit, because the Spirit intercedes for the saints in accordance with God's will" (Rom. 8:27).

197   "Pray without ceasing. In everything we give thanks, for this is the will of God in Christ Jesus for you" (1 Thess. 5:17–18).

198   James 1:6; faithlessness contrasts maturity and show the faithless as having no spiritual standing. A faithless person is incompetent of winning spiritual warfare.

understanding of the trinity. The concept does not in any way suggest that the Son is inferior to the Father. All three persons of the trinity are equal in deity; the ranking is a theological construct and relates to function. The Father is supreme; the Son carries out the Father's will through the Holy Spirit.[199] Jesus prefers to act through the Father because of who He is. As the Spirit of truth, He helps people do the Father's will. Jesus Christ is the most significant symbol of prayer.

Jesus' indwelling presence does not set aside the need to worship God in temples made of brick. Thoughtful prayer is as suitable for worship as prayer verbally done in a temple. Refuting the argument of the Samaritan woman, Jesus answered,

> *It is no longer necessary to claim a single mountain as the only holy place to pray to God.*[200]

God is better served in places where justice is ruler, and by showing the truth of every heart in holiness:

> *The time has come when the true worshippers will worship the Father in spirit and in truth, for they are the kind of worshippers the Father seeks. God is Spirit and His worshippers must worship Him in spirit and in truth.*[201]

---

199   John 5:19; "My food is to do the will of Him who sent me, and to finish his work" (John 4:34).

200   "Sir," The woman said to Jesus, "Our fathers worshipped on this mountain (Mount Gerizim), but you Jews claim that the place where we must worship is in Jerusalem." Jesus answered, "Believe me; time is coming when you will worship the Father neither on this mountain nor in Jerusalem" (John 4:19–21).

201   John 4:23–24

A prayerful Christian is a powerful Christian. Through prayer, the Church resists Satan's assaults and seeks ways out of serious spiritual problems. Prayer is an open door to receiving gifts of grace, healing, and deliverance.[202] It helps to build trust in God and can relax a worrying mind.

Prayer is an effective way to know God. Private prayer emphasizes intimacy and gathers conviction that God is truly personal. A personal God may not easily be realized by simply taking part in corporate prayer. The thoughts of Psalm 63 are the concern of the lonely condition in which David called God, my God.[203]

Hiding from his enemies in the desert of Judah, David felt intensely lonely. He longed for a friend he could trust to ease the loneliness, so he cried out to God. I appreciate all aspects of Psalm 63, especially the way David claimed God. The prayer demonstrates that God has interpersonal qualities; and by this means, I am immensely favored. David played like music the genuineness of his heart desire, expressing how he forever wanted to belong to God. He was filled with adoring emotion as he called on God to favor his deep concern. God's salvation is a personal gift to David as it is to all true believers. Lonely times like sleepless nights, illness, and worry can be turned into quiet times of reflection and worship. Using lonely times to review God's guidance, we may discover more of His loving kindness.

We must not seek to remain in lonely conditions but should always seek to unite our sacrifice of praise, petition, and intercession with those of the band of fellow believers. We have a God who

---

202   Eph. 6: 13; Matt. 26: 41

203   "Oh God, you are my God; early will I seek you; my soul thirsts for you; my flesh longs for you in a dry and thirsty land where there is no water. So I have looked for you in the sanctuary to see your power and your glory; because your loving-kindness is better than life. I will praise you" (Ps. 63:1–3).

befriends us in all faithfulness; He surrounds us with a cloud of witness; the angels and the saints in the Church triumph. The apostle John said,

> *How great is the love the Father lavished on us, that we are called children of God. And that is what we are.*[204]
> *Those who obey His commands live in Him, and He in them. And this is how we know that He lives in us; we know it by the Spirit He gave us.*[205]

God will answer anyone who seeks Him in earnest, for He is God to all who seek His salvation.[206] By praying like David did, you may assume the spirit through whom David claimed God. And by an overwhelmingly sensitive conscience, you could totally be overtaken by the awareness that God has already declared His active love the evidence of your salvation. David felt God's active love when he longed for deliverance, and the love motivated him to pray.

The apostle Peter said,

> *The eyes of the Lord are on the righteous, and His ears are attentive to their cry.*[207]

God hears the prayers of the righteous and responds according to the cry of those who respect Him. He sees the heart of all men whether they have truly been born of His Spirit.

---

204   1 John 3:1

205   1 John 3:24

206   "'Then you will call upon me and come and pray to me, and I will listen to you. You will seek me and find me when you seek me with all your heart. Then I will be found by you,' declares the Lord" (Jer. 29:12–14).

207   1 Pet. 3:7; Ps. 34:15

So far in this chapter—as it is the discussion of *Constants of Delightful Worship* as a whole—I have described the fill details of prayer according to a singular theme—that worshipful prayer must be both a corporate and private exercise. These are two aspects of prayer that the Bible addresses. Each aspect has unique relevance; and all good prayers fall into the category.

Prayer by the dead is not biblical. Therefore, the claim that the dead pray for the living has no part in this book's discussion.[208] What is the point in consulting the dead for the sake of the living?

In the face of crises that can result in impatience and for lack of trust in God's word, some children of God push themselves into many troubles by thinking about holy things in unholy ways and by using unholy means toward holy ends. Consulting the dead is against the command of the sovereign Lord. Prophet Isaiah said,

When they say to you "Seek those who are mediums and wizards, who whisper and mutter," should not a people seek their God? Should they seek the dead on behalf of the living?[209]

Isaiah's verdict is that, in no circumstance, must God's people accept spiritual counsel from anyone who does not speak according to God's word. You ought to trust in God for guidance; God knows the future, and only He is eternal. Nothing else, other than communion with the living God, either privately or in group, is genuinely considered prayer.

Private prayer benefits the one saying it more than others; the one saying private prayer is, at the time, the only spotlight in God's eyes.

---

208   "The living knows that they will die, but the dead know nothing. Their memory left them and their love, envy, and hatred are now perished; nevermore will they have a share in anything done under the sun" (Eccles. 9:5–6).

209   Isa. 8:19

Group prayer is equally effective as private prayer. Group prayer serves the unity of the Church; it is the manifestation of a desire to worship God jointly and the means to lift joint burden and praise to heaven. Group prayer benefits all of the involved in similar ways; the exercise is like the lending of hands. Praying in a group creates understanding by promoting love among God's children. Praying with one voice reinforces expectations for positive outcome. Unity of faith is unity of strength, and unity of strength is unity of love. Communal need may likely generate more compassion if everyone joins hands to pray.

The story of Nineveh in the book of Jonah is an outstanding example of the power of communal prayer. God planned to destroy the city of Nineveh because of its multitude of sin, and He sent Prophet Jonah to openly proclaim His plan in the city. The king of Nineveh was troubled by the news, and in response, he declared three days of fasting and prayer for everyone in the city, including the animals. Nineveh's submission made eligible their supplication in asking God's forgiveness. God accepted their prayer and forgive their sin.[210] The city of Nineveh was, at the time, spared because all of its citizens took God's word seriously. The people responded with sincere hearts, and together, they fasted and prayed.

Changing God's mind in a boiling situation like that in Nineveh would probably have been difficult if only a few of its citizens had prayed for the sins of the entire city. The pleas of a few persons would possibly have achieved the safe exit of their immediate families before the rest of the city perished. This was the case when Sodom and Gomorrah was destroyed and only Lot and his family were saved.[211] Abraham intervened for Sodom and Gomorrah but failed to hold back God's anger, which blazed toward the wickedness of the

---

210   Jonah 3
211   Gen. 18:16; Gen. 19:1–29; the rest people of the city and the city itself were erased with fire.

people. Sodom and Gomorrah perished because the people jointly failed to repent.[212]

The lesson of Nineveh is obvious, and we are hunted by our own arrogance. A life of abundance is God's gift to every nation that repents, and God alone can execute a standing judgment. The attitude of the messenger to Nineveh seems to imply that Nineveh did not deserve mercy. But God considered Nineveh's supplication with mercy and allowed the people a good measure of His grace.

Sometimes people wish that destruction would come upon sinful people whose wickedness seems to demand immediate judgment. But God has the greatest concern for the world; He rebukes such hardness and proclaims His willingness to save everyone. Never underestimate the Lord's mercy and His willingness to forgive. Never discourage repentance, and do not grieve when your enemy decides to repent and, therefore, to escape the judgment you may feel that he or she deserve. God's compassion is not only for Israel, the chosen nation, but for the entire human race. He takes no pleasure in the death of the wicked but desires everyone to turn away from evil and live.[213]

Having bestowed on the world His great and compassionate love, Jesus Christ encouraged the world to shape its character according to the inward knowledge of righteousness. The Church of Christ all over the world must wake up to pray; Christians languish when they do not pray. Mutual fasting and prayer could, on behalf of common good, produce more positive results than the prayer of a few people.

I am not saying emphatically that one person's prayer cannot solve communal problem. God alone answers prayer, and He

---

212   Gen. 18:16–33

213   Ezek. 33:11, "The Lord answered Jonah, ;But Nineveh has more than a hundred and twenty thousand people who cannot tell their right from their left, and many cattle as well. Should I not be concerned about that great city?'" (Jonah 4:11).

determines the legitimacy of any prayer. My point is that the prayer of an entire nation is likely to be more effective than the prayer of a few of its citizens.

Corporate prayer can be classified in two different ways. Corporate prayer can mean prayer involving a group of people. The group may gather at a time to pray, as such gathering can be arranged during Church service or when there is common purpose for one or more worship groups to gather to pray. Corporate prayer can also mean prayer in which everyone involved is at a different location at a given time but is respectively praying for the same goal within the hour. Under the latter condition, those united in prayer are away from each other physically while focusing their prayer and fasting on an agreed-upon subject.

Prayer does not mean indiscriminate talk; good prayer requires an orderly presentation. An ideal prayer begins with a confession of faith and incorporates praise and thanksgiving by acknowledging God for His mighty deeds in view of His creation and goodness in giving everyone the grace of life.

Confession of faith is followed by confession of sin, which incorporates an acknowledgment of human weakness. One should offer such a declaration, especially that of personal failure, not as an excuse but as reality and must support an honest plea for God's mercy and forgiveness. A good Christian relates confession of sin to the sins of the world by asking not just for personal vindication. Biblical spirituality does not entail withdrawal from the world's turmoil but, rather, identification with the world in its shame and affliction. It is important to mention the reality of universal sin in prayer. Jesus Christ desires to help the world repent in order to save all people. Nonbelievers may consider repenting when they see that they are at fault. By your prayer, the Holy Spirit can provoke such awareness.

In the final steps of prayer, worshippers present need and make intercessions that could overcome those needs.

Closure implies a unifying appeal for everything said in the prayer—God's grace, good health, and open doors. Jesus Christ is our Lord and mediator before God; therefore, prayer is concluded in the name of Jesus Christ our Lord and sealed with the expression *amen*, which translates to "let it be as it is said."

Christian Faith and World Instability
Christian faith is absolute if it proceeds from the faithfulness of God. An absolute faith derives its value by expressing itself in acts of love. Acting by love requires spiritual maturity; the ability to do so is the mark of effective Christians.

Recommending the Church of Thessalonica for their act of love, the apostle Paul wrote,

> *We continually remember before our God and Father your work produced by faith, your labor prompted by love, and your endurance inspired by hope in our Lord Jesus Christ.*[214]

The distinguishing quality of an absolute faith is generally identified in the New Testament as faith, which in practice is not merely unfounded, wishful thinking but hope and love expressed steadfastly to God's will. We freely exercise faith because faith is an attitude derived of God's Spirit within us, which is God's gift to us. In relation to Christ's work, such faith renders repentance hopeful in that, through faith, God's forgiveness is real and achievable. Loving is an act of faith; and we can received faith through hearing God's spoken word.[215] Faith is our ethical response to God's grace. Without faith, pleasing God is impossible.[216]

---

214   1 Thess. 1:3
215   Rom. 10:17
216   Heb. 11:6

Faith may sound abstract in a certain way, but it is living water to those who thirst for God and bread to those who hunger in Him,

For the message of the Cross is foolishness to those who are perishing, but to those who are being saved, it is the power of God.[217]

True faith is not static; human suffering affects all people in similar ways, and the condition warrants that a mindless believer can fall out of faith. Hence, an ideal faith is renewable; it helps the spirit to grow and continue the struggle.

We find an example of such faith in Abraham. Through several difficult experiences, Abraham learned to mature his trust in God. He managed his faith well when God tested him, asking him to offer his son, Isaac, on the altar. By all account, Abraham's faith is accounted to him for righteousness. The apostle James regards Abraham as a friend of God because of Abraham's faith in God.[218]

Faith and hope works together, but each work toward a slightly different end. An empty religion will betray itself in relationship to faith by defining saving faith as simply the claim of hope or merely the acceptance of a creed. Your faith sustains your hope for the things you ask for; and by faith, you produce an obedient life that will allow you to receive all of God's promises. Hope cannot stand without the support of a living faith. Faith is like

---

217   1 Cor. 1:18–19; Isa. 29:14; God promised to do marvelous things in the life of His people if His people will continually seek Him, expressing wholeheartedly trust in Him. His wondrous work will finally bring shame to the understanding of this world; and the earthly wisdom will be brought to nothing.

218   James 2:22–23

pillar by which hope exists. However, faith does not solely require the support of hope to succeed. Hope ceases when it accomplishes its expectation, but saving faith survives forever. The apostle Paul said,

> For we are saved in this hope. But hope that is seen is no hope at all. Who hopes for what he already has? But if we hope for what we do not yet have, we eagerly wait for it with the perseverance of faith.[219]

It is useless to pray without faith. You must believe that God hears your prayer and will sufficiently reward you. When you have no specific need to lift up your prayer, remember that your daily breath warrants thanksgiving:

> Be joyful always; pray continually; give thanks in all circumstances, for this is God's will for you in Christ Jesus.[220]

If you lack consistency in your prayer regiment, not making prayer a habit, you may put out the Spirit of fire within you. Faith is an essential, indispensable element of prayer.

God's answer to prayer comes through many means. He absolutely controls the rewards we may receive, but this does not mean that one may not receive an outright response. Answer to prayer can be instant and spontaneous, but the result may take time to manifest. Even when the result of our prayer is delayed, God

---

219   Rom. 8:24–25

220   1 Thess. 5:16–18; "When you were dead in your sins and in the circumcision of your sinful nature, God made you alive with Christ. He forgave us all our sins, having canceled the written code with its regulations that was against us and that stood opposed to us; He took it away, nailing it to the cross" (1 Thess. 2:13–14).

does not overlook the cause.[221] This implies that when and how God responds to prayer absolutely depends on Him. Your responsibility is to pray in faith; your request is, in essence, the means for God to respond.

Faith commands patience and acknowledgment that God perceives every human condition, and in each case, He decides what is best for His children. The knowledge that God know what is best explains, in part, why God may instantly grant a prayerful request while delaying or presumably denying another. God's method is not mathematic. "No" is a valid answer to prayer, and God's "no" shares the same capacity of His "yes." God may decide to keep you waiting in order to test your faith. He may reward your prayer with a gift that you did not ask for, knowing that what you asked will not serve the situation well.

In all circumstance, prayer works for the good of those who trust in God—those who are called according to His purpose.[222] God answers many prayers in ways that are difficult to understand—sometimes in ways that can neither be seen with ordinary eyes nor explained by any human logic.

Nevertheless, the difficulty in accepting certain decision by God does not equal ambiguity, which some Christians create by praying to God while they listen to their emotions for answers. Such an attitude is nearly equal to idol worship; those Christians, thereby, forsake God's purpose concerning their case. We must learn to work

---

221 "Then He continued, 'Do not be afraid, Daniel. Since the first day that you set your mind to gain understanding and humble yourself before God, your words were heard, and I have come in response to them. But the prince of the Persian kingdom resisted me twenty-one days. Then Michael, one of the chief princes, came to help me, because I was detained there with the king of Persia. Now I have come to explain to you what will happen to your people in the future, for the vision concerns a time yet to come'" (Dan. 10:12–14).

222 Rom. 8:28

with God's lead, despite how confusing His lead may sometimes seem. Human life is more complex than it ordinarily seems. We require patience and discernment to follow God's path.

Some of Jesus' talk about prayer and faith seemed strange to His disciples. There is more to life in the spirit realm than there is to things on the surface. Strange as some of His words may also seem to us, be assured that Jesus is certain about what He says. He came out of the unseen world perfectly familiar with the forces that play behind veil, which we know nothing about.

In all, prayer is our greatest resource. In preparing our hope, faith must supersede all doubt. Christians should neither grow weary in waiting for God's answer to prayer nor reject God's lead the way it is.

Those who hopefully wait in the Lord shall not be disappointed.[223] *Even youths grow tired and weary, and young men stumble and fall; but those who hope in the Lord will renew their strength.*[224]

Every generation is caught up in its own problem and cleverness, but God's plan embraces all generations. God holds in His hands the workings and interworkings of the forces of the universe. He brings into play extraordinary power to supplement those that we know about. Trusting God requires relying on Him, even when we do not understand the reason for certain outcomes. God's vision will not delay longer than is necessary.

The revelation waits an appointed time. It speaks of the end, and will not prove false. Though it linger, wait for it; it will certainly come.[225]

---

223   Isa. 49:23
224   Isa. 40:30–31
225   Hab. 2:3

By contrast, not all prayer is genuine; only a few prayers are made in righteousness. Prayer should not be of evil intent; God does not assist wickedness. God's answer to prayer is totally negative when one has not asked in righteousness and according to His divine will. God does not contradict His word; He is holy and serves justice.

On the journey to the Promised Land, Moses prayed to cross over the River Jordan with the remnant of the house of Israel, but because of His anger toward Moses, God said to him,

That's enough; do not speak to me anymore about this matter[226]

God allowed Moses the opportunity to see the land; He told Moses to go up to the edge of plateau Pisgah, which overlook the Death Sea. In Pisgah, Moses saw the land before he died.[227]

This story demonstrates that negligence and anger can hinder prayer.[228] We learn God's character by reviewing His actions in history. Thus, we can avoid mistakes in our own lives by understanding the mistakes of earlier worshippers.

Again, God's answer to prayer is negative when His can better reveal to you His glory and grace by means of you going through a trial, instead of being rescued from the trial. The apostle Paul told the Church of Corinth about his share of enduring suffering in order that God is glorified through him:

---

226   Deut. 3:26–28

227   Num. 21:20

228   Deut. 1:37–38; "Because of you the Lord became angry with me also and said, 'You shall not enter it (the land) either. But your assistant, Joshua son of Nun, will lead Israel to inherit it'" (Num. 20:9–13). Out of anger, Moses failed to honor the Lord's instruction when he struck the rock at Meribah twice to give water to the people. God was also angry toward Israel for inciting Moses to sin.

Concerning these things, I pleaded with the Lord three times that it might depart from me and He said to me, "My grace is sufficient for you, for my strength is made perfect in weakness." Therefore, most gladly, I will boast in my infirmities that the power of Christ may rest upon me.[229]

God had a better solution than to remove Paul's problem; he relied on the likelihood that human weakness would, at times, provide the ideal opportunity for a display of God's divinity and justice.

The unseen power of faith is courage; and Paul is not the only biblical person who had such an experience. In Gethsemane, Jesus prayed in the hour before His arrest,

O My Father, if it is possible, let this cup pass from me; nevertheless, not as I will but as you will.[230]

God greeted Jesus' prayer with silence. Jesus had to go through the torture and pain that was to come in order that He accomplished His task of the cross in the flesh.

From the moment of His arrest and all the way to the cross, Jesus suffered in obedience to the Father. We know that His suffering was the Father's will; the episode was revealed in the law and foretold by the prophets. Jesus agonized not because of fear of His impending physical death, but because of the weight of human transgression that He would endure. As a result, His holy nature shrank from the thought.

The end result of His suffering is an everlasting glory and honor to the Father who sent Him. Concerning the reason God sent His Son to suffer death, Isaiah wrote,

---

229   2 Cor. 12:8–9
230   Matt. 26:39

Yet it pleased the Lord to bruise Him; He has put Him to grief.
When you make His soul an offering for sin, He shall see His
seed, He shall prolong His days, and the pleasure of the Lord
shall prosper in His hand. He shall see the labor of His soul,
and be satisfied. By His knowledge, my righteous Servant shall
justify many, for He shall bear their iniquities.[231]

It is gratifying that the servant have faithfully served the master. Those who are saved are not saved by any human effort but by Jesus' work of righteousness. Every believer ought to return God's love with faithfulness. Each believer's salvation is justified by his or her claim of Christ's deed.

We must trust our God in every way and in whichever means He works miracle in our life. Worship, especially prayer, is a relationship of trust; the practice calls for openness of heart. We must accept God's judgment with thanksgiving, even when we feel sad about certain outcomes of life's situations. God Himself is the standard of justice. He uses His power according to His own moral perfection. Whatever He does is fair, even when we do not understand His purpose.

Our best response to life's circumstances is to appeal directly to Him; thus to pray is to discern God's mind. People often add God's approval as a rubber stamp to their actions—to something they have already determined to do.

We may question certain of life's circumstances, but we must have faith that God is in control. We must work with faith in both pleasant and difficult times so as to effectively serve God. Christians who do not accept God's judgment for an answer to prayer are likely to stop praying. Their trust in God is likely to collapse because their attitude asks God to accept human will. Prayer does not guarantee that you will always get what you ask; but it does guarantee that what

---

231   Isa. 53:10–11

happens will be what's best for every situation. The relationship of prayer is like a stewardship; you get what you need for your spiritual and physical survival, not all that you desire. Prayer renews the spirit of our mind as part of the process toward becoming Christlike.[232]

By renewing your mind, you are being transformed—making every thought captive to obedience to Christ.[233] Jesus said,

> *Do not worry about your life, saying "What shall we eat or what shall we drink or what shall we wear," for the unbelievers run after these things, and your heavenly Father knows that you need them. Do not worry about tomorrow, for tomorrow will worry about its own things. Each day's trouble is sufficient for it.*[234]

It is sometimes difficult to connect these words fully to real-life situations. However, prayer guides our plan for the future, and living with such trust is a time well spent. God provides for every living thing that He caused to exist; therefore worrying is time wasted. Worriers, by contrast, are consumed by fear, and they find it difficult to trust in God.

Obstacles to Prayer

Suffering begins with setbacks that cling to the worldliness of every age. Among the many ways that people may lose out for not having faith in prayer, worldliness accounts for all major obstacles to prayerfulness. Worldliness is the aspect of secularism that sees life as an end in itself, which helps keep desperation on the rise. Secularism and perversion seriously endanger all exercise of spirituality, just as not fighting back diminishes many people's hope that they may emerge victorious in the struggle.

---

232   Eph. 4:23
233   Rom. 12:2
234   Matt. 6:31–32; Matt. 6:34

Our prayers are crucial to our survival because our best praying will move us into our best action. The Gospel admits the difficult time we live in but insists that a successful Christian life is practicable. In this case, trial of faith is different from suffering caused by worldliness. Especially in 1 Peter, trial of faith and glory are repeatedly paired. Partakers of Christ's suffering will rejoice with exceeding joy at the revelation of His glory. Peter is so passionate about triumph over this world that he considers the trial of faith more precious than gold.

Be armed for suffering; feed your inner mind with God's word, and you will survive the tragedies of this life. I have learned by experience how faith in God provides the means to serve difficult occasion. If living through the struggles of this life can give to all people the satisfying thirst of true goodness, the work of faith is done. To me, the kindness of Church community is outstanding. By personal effort and the assistance of the Holy Spirit, my struggle and my part in teaching and preaching the Bible speaks of God's power at work.

Fear of the world's unpredictability is a reality, and the effect of unbelief is unhelpful. But nothing of this imperfect world can measure the treasures we can find in God. When we lived by the rule of God's, we somehow incorporate the rule of our regular system as well. The difference is that secular people trust only in their ability to excel, but with prayer, God's children add their trust in the Lord's name.[235] The democratic system of the current world is set to allow everyone the freedom to conduct his or her life in his or her own way and cleverness; it allows us to surround ourselves to the environment with which we can identify. But the system is a delusion of reality. Only a few people grasp the reality of life, while the majority chases after illusion. The apostle Peter made clear how believers can segregate themselves from popular lifestyle; he called the Church a living stone being built into

---

235   "Some trust in chariots and some in horses, but we trust in the name of the Lord our God" (Ps. 20:7).

a spiritual house.[236] Every believer is a stone and Jesus Christ is the capstone. One stone is not the house but part of the house, and one stone is virtually nothing without the others.

In his second letter, Peter further emphasized the Church as a unique community, showing how growth begins with faith and concludes in love for others. It is helpful to join forces with other Christians, especially in prayer. Peter's explanation works for us by showing that, when God calls you to a task, He also calls other people to work with you. God's resources are infinite, and He completes your joy by giving you encouragement. Joining your footsteps alongside the footsteps of other believers will multiply your efforts. As part of a Church community, your initiative will not appeal to unbelievers' worldview.

The world is a stage on which everyone plays a part, but biblically speaking, the manner in which people desire things and worry about their desire is callous. Over-ambition drains many lives. Jesus asked,

What will it profit a man, if he gains everything he wants from this world but at the end loses his soul?[237]

Knowing that whatever we own on Earth is temporal and cannot be exchanged for our soul, Jesus speaks out against those who desire to contain their destiny within their resolve—those who often base their self-concept on personal accomplishment.

Your true worth is that you are one of God's children; no earthly treasure can equal the worth of your life. God's children have the grace to live and the grace to die. The flesh is crucified so that the spirit may forever live. Endeavor to find joy through prayer in moments you suffer grief. People tend to have short memory when it comes to God's

---

236   1 Peter 2
237   Mark 8:36–37

faithfulness, but prayer coordinates all memories of the Lord's doing. We need to remind ourselves of the wondrous works of God and carry each other's burden through the teaching of prayer shared among all Churches and their members. Jesus taught His disciples to pray[238] so that every believer can expand the use of prayer to enrich the common good. The Holy Spirit is the miracle worker, and the Church under His control is capable of opening many closed doors. Otherwise,

> *The kingdom of heaven is like a dragnet that was cast into the sea and gathered some of every kind, which when it was full, they drew it to shore, and they sat down and gathered the good into vessels, but threw the bad away. So it shall be at the end of ages. The angels will come forth; separate the wicked from among the just.*[239]

Divide in Christendom

From conception, every person has the freedom to pledge a good conscience to God. We are in no way compelled by the rule of God's law. God knows that every inclination of a human heart is evil from birth, yet He chooses to love us in order to save us from the compelling evil. The season is a reminder of God's promise to Noah[240] never to coerce humanity to obey and worship Him.[241]

The occasion of our life is testing our righteousness. We are neither threatened by God's commandment nor compelled by the danger of hellfire to love and worship God. God appreciates only worship that comes from a willing heart. He does not despise a

---

238   Matt. 6:9–13 – the Lord's Prayer

239   Matt. 13:47–49 – the parable of the dragnet

240   "Never again will I curse the ground because of man, even though every inclination of his heart is evil from childhood. And never again will I destroy all living creatures as I have done. As long as the earth endures, seedtime and harvest, cold and winter, day and night will never cease" (Gen. 8:21–22).

241   Gen. 6–7

broken and repentant heart, and He does not delight in an outward sacrifice. The Bible is simply a guide, helping us to conduct our life and cleverness in order to gain the righteousness of God. It is in our interest to set sinning aside and uplift our spirit to prevail over our natural, sinful bodies. By righteousness we are in peace with God, even though it does not profit God that we are righteous. With righteousness, everyone is profitable to himself.[242]

Jesus made it possible for all people to enter God's sanctuary and safely stand before the throne of God's presence not having the fear of death. At the time of Jesus' death on the cross, the sun stopped shining and darkness reigned for three hours. God allowed darkness to settle on the foulest moment in history, when Jesus stood alone, enduring the pain of hell so as to keep us from the experience. The curtain separating the holiest part of the temple split in the moment that Jesus died, thereby allowing whoever worships God to worship Him face-to-face. Premeditated, the event honors personal accountability in a celebration of spiritual liberation that is central to redemption.[243]

---

242   "Can a man be profitable to God, though he who is wise may be profitable to himself? Is it any pleasure to the Almighty that you are righteous? Or is it gain to Him that you make your ways blameless?" (Job 22:1–3).

243   Luke 23:45; when Jesus drew His last breathe on the Cross, the temple curtain of the most holy place tore into parts. Christ opened the way into God's presence. The old system of worship ceased to be upon the temple high priest, on whom the honor is bestowed to enter the most holy place on behalf of God's worshippers. In Heb. 9:2–5 and Heb. 9:8–9, a description of the holiest place and the significance of the torn curtain were given as follows: "A tabernacle was set up; in its first room were the lamp-stand, the table, and the consecrated bread. Behind the second curtain was a room called the Most Holy Place, it had the golden altar of incense and the gold-covered Ark of the Covenant. The Ark contained the gold jar of Manna, Aaron's staff that had budded, and the stone tablets of the covenant. Above the Ark were the Cherubim of the Glory, overshadowing the atonement cover. The Holy Spirit was showing by this that the way into the Most Holy Place had not yet been disclosed as long as the first tabernacle was still standing."

According to the apostle Paul,

That power is like the working of God's strength, which He exerted in Jesus Christ when He raised Him from the dead, and seated Him at His right hand side in the heavenly realms, far above all principalities and powers of darkness.[244]

Having perceived firsthand the determination of the spiritual hosts of darkness against the Church, Paul predicted similar victory for Christ's resurrection, saying that the hope of the Church is not a vague feeling that the future will be positive. The challenge persists, but the completed work of Jesus' victory is the Church's complete assurance.

It is particularly irrelevant whether the opponent at the present time is a principality, a powerful ruler of darkness of this age, or both. We may be confident that, whichever is the case, its power is limited, it will endure for only a certain time frame, and it belongs to a spiritually organized army ranked under the lordship of Satan. Though not using the same term as Paul, I refer to the in-house powers working against the Church as "denominational kingdom."

Paul noticed beforehand that many people freely enter God's presence, but only a few take home His grace in honor. He warned that God's grace would not withstand His judgment:

Do not be deceived; God cannot be mocked. A man reaps what he sows. The one who sows to please his sinful nature, from that nature will reap destruction; the one who sows to please the Spirit, from the Spirit will reap eternal life.[245]

---

244   Eph. 1:19–21

245   Gal. 6:7–8, the law of 'sow and reap' applies to every one. Sow only those seed you desire to reap; for God has guaranteed that His judgment will surely come to pass.

We do not achieve godliness by merely observing an external code of conduct; rather, we achieve it by living through the word, the helmet of salvation, and the sword of the Spirit.[246] For material and repulsive interests, some people among the community of worshippers are like wolf in sheep's clothing. The rulers of darkness use them to divert the course of God's kingdom to reflect a form of denominational kingdom. The paradox implies the pursuit of secret ambition within the Church against a common goal, which is access to the kingdom of heaven.

For denominational kingdom worshippers, God's house of worship serves as cover for occult practice. Those who shelter the concept have a mind-set that is open to occult power and self-centered service. These men and women believe that the Church is a double-edged mythological body; they see the Church's gathering as spiritually symbolic and assume that members may worship any spirit of their choice. The people involved exist in secret union and support only programs that promote the material interest of the Church. At the moment, fancy programs account for entertainment in Church, overriding the true heart of spiritual worship.

Denominational kingdom evolved from the pagan idea of Church and State tied to one authority, which in the Greek era of the ancient Roman Empire allowed the mainstream of Christian worshippers to indulge in idol worship. Occultism is witchcraft; never mind that the concept is attracting different definition and cultural modification from several public arenas. The practice existed in many parts of the world before Christianity was born.

Scripture tells of the Jewish leadership's initiation of the plot that crucified Jesus Christ. One may argue that God destined His Son's death the way it is carried out, but it is ironic that leaders of God's holy temple are the forerunners of the plot. Despite the argument

---

246   Eph. 6:17

about who killed Jesus, occultism mixed with religiosity and the use of Church for other gain has caused many serious problems. Occultism was partly responsible for both the First World War and the Second World War, as it is responsible for some of the modern-day problems, such as the so-called War on Terrorism.

A more disturbing aspect of the danger is that denominational kingdom worshippers rule the world; Paul mentioned these people as rulers of the darkness of this age. Since the first Church split of the Middle Ages, Christians have, inevitably, lived through more splits. It is admissible as fact that, despite many odd squabbles, the Church has continued to advance the Gospel. However, Paul's concern then, which has since been realized, was that those rulers would highjack certain Christian minds and that such associations with the dark world would increasingly cause global damage to the Christian faith. Christianity served colonialism, the slave trade, and Nazism. At present, Christianity is caught in between intimidation and bloodshed that damages the global goal to gain more souls for Christ. The twenty-first century is witnessing high levels of confusion surrounding belief; and spirituality is worsening. Widespread hatred of the Jewish nation creates resentment toward the fundamental message of the Gospel, while Christians are being murdered around the world. These are part of the damages denominational kingdom worshippers have caused; their association with the Church is, in no small measure, setting the stage for the battle of Armageddon.[247]

It is more likely that the Antichrist will emerge either among Jews or the Church; and more people are likely to go down the grill if that should happen. The Antichrist's pattern of deceit will

---

247   Rev. 16:16, the battle will be the last between the forces of good and evil. Armageddon is prophesied as the battlefield, a land mass near the city of Megiddo in Northern Israel. Sinful people will unite to fight against God in a final display of rebellion. The gathering takes shape, and is intended against Christ and His people.

cause many to fall prey to more satanic ideology. Paul's perception of denominational kingdom joins the New Testament idea that the spirit of the antichrist will manifest in many ways, both within and outside the Church, and will finally culminate in one person or an institution or both. Therefore,

> *Watch out that you do not lose what you worked for, but that we may receive a full reward. Anyone who transgresses and does not abide in the doctrine of Christ does not have God. Whoever abides in the doctrine of Christ has both the Father and the Son. If anyone comes to you and does not bring this teaching, do not take him into your house or welcome him. Anyone who welcomes him shares in his wicked work.*[248]

Some maintain that we can only believe in God in spite of experience as we walk by faith, not by sight. This view forgets that walking by faith is an experience. We should not be suspicious about every member of the Church, but we need to be wise in evaluating the conduct and character of those who could falsely seek to influence the Church. It is necessary from the beginning to "test" the spirits to see if they are from God in terms of their effect on love, truth, and unity in the fellowship.[249]

Christianity is a way of life to experience and not just a theory to believe. False teaching is a serious affair, and we dare not overlook it. Christians should define the twenty-first century for what it is, rather than accepting the time as an era of the so-called scientific Christianity. The twenty-first century is, in part, peopled by a generation of impostors—those who undermine the foundation and true benefit of faith by applying right words to other meaning. It is their saying that,

248   2 John 8–11
249   1 John 4

behind every masterpiece, is the master who created the piece, yet they advocate the "big bang" as the origin of the universe.

Walk only in the truth; love to please God, not people; and beware of those who act presumptuously against God's commandments. The modern attitude toward the Bible is profoundly influenced by Martin Luther and John Calvin. These great reformers never intended that the right of every individual to read the Bible should mean that individuals have the right to stand in judgment upon scripture or make decisions about the Bible according to their own private interpretations. Rather, they insist that every individual must make a personal response to God's word, which scripture contains.

False teachers claim superior knowledge in order to contradict the original meaning of the biblical writers and the apostolic doctrine, but God's Spirit leads those who align themselves with Him to the truth. We read the Bible for our inspiration and profit, which contributes vastly to the fulfillment of the ambition of the reformers. To this end, you should discover this season as a season that seriously asks for your prayer and devotion in things of God. May the minds of God's people move away from the events of this era that His people may focus only on the truth of His kingdom. In this modern time, faith serves merely as a tradition and symbol of national unity against any foreign society. To another, faith is a political tool for imperialism—a gateway to invade people's liberty.

As the popularity of fanaticism, nationalism, and secularism increases among many worldview, the Church fail to represent a people of one mission and principle. A variety of interests exist within the Church because the Church isn't one. This adds to the opinion that secular voices could speak better for many national affairs than spiritual voices. Again, we must learn from false prophets of the old—how they fooled themselves, not God. The false prophets prophesied only what ambitious kings and people wanted to hear. They were hailed, but in the end they sold out their souls.

In the name of redefining worship, each of the past generations suffered either from not knowing what to believe or not being sure of what to practice. The current generation confronts a worse form of moral problem, suffering from knowing neither what to believe nor what to practice. Complexity has resulted in moral chaos. This complexity has no real explanation, except that the current generation has based worship on the activities of the flesh. Despite the alleged good, a worship pattern built upon the flesh is of no benefit to the spirit. Worship by the flesh will neither please God nor stand the test of time. Debates about subjects like human homosexuality and divine femininity do not result from scriptural ambiguity about true worship; these are hypotheses that have arisen from the present situation. Such debates are increasingly popular because those in favor of change have the tendency to transform worship into whatever they desire. The Bible gives plenty of hints concerning the good in using the spirit to control the outer body. But for whatever reason, homosexuals believe in an illusion that allows them to justify the body above the spirit. The voices of nature, the Scripture, and tradition unite in constant condemnation of all homosexual acts:

Do not lie with a man as one lies with a woman; that is detestable. Do not have sexual relationship with an animal and defile yourself with it. A woman must not present herself to an animal to have sexual relations with it; that is a perversion. Do not defile yourselves in any of these ways, because this is how the nation that I am going to drive out before you became defiled.[250]

---

250   Lev. 18:22–24

If the defense of homosexual acts relies upon love, the Bible does not teach that erotic love supplements agape.[251] And neither can erotic love find fulfillment in the context of agape. We read,

Love does not delight in evil, but rejoices with the truth.[252]

Homosexuals confuse love with lust. Love that gets its way by covert scam is simply a psychological game; it does not proceed from a heart of love, and it is not directed to bless and seek the partners' highest good. Godlike love stands in total contrast to all secular ideas of love, of which homosexuality is a member:

Do you not know that the wicked will not inherit the kingdom of God? Do not be deceived: Neither the sexually immoral nor idolaters nor adulterers nor male prostitutes nor homosexual offenders nor thieves nor the greedy nor drunkards nor slanderers nor swindlers will inherit the kingdom of God.[253]

Modern redefinition of worship is justifiable with disobedience in the same way that false prophets existed among the prophets of the ancient time. We do not deny the existence of unbelieving ministers of the Gospel and churchgoers amid devoted Christians; even the apostles encountered a false preacher named Bar Jesus.[254] The ministers who serve in disobedience are the modern-day false prophets; they serve by sentiment and, thereby, refuse to condemn corrupt practices. By delusive examples, false teachers are sending many good followers to the wrong grave. I hardly argue in my writing that the rebellious and ridiculous practices, such as ordaining gay priests and allowing

251   Eph. 5:21–32
252   1 Cor. 13:6
253   1 Cor. 6:9–11
254   Acts 13:6

gay marriage; to do so may help to further the satanic opinion. The problem is not the oneness of God in diverse culture, but the diverse human approach. The diverse approach chiefly constitutes an earthly wisdom and serves no true benefit to spirituality.

Except by the Bible, other forms of approach to God is fraud. Scientific truth is particularly conditional. The modern overriding criticism of the Bible and doubt about the source and authenticity should deter no serious believer. The intention is to equal God and idol, which secular voices hope to achieve by engaging the argument. Notably, theology and religion have no equal standing, and science is not spiritually based. Christians should not reject certain religious and scientific concepts, except to match them to their worth.

More ridiculous are the anti-miracle scientists, who examine spiritual things by material means. These scientists openly doubt the truthfulness of the Bible and the genuineness of works of faith, yet they devote all energy that money can mobilize investigating and replicating biblical stories and events. According to Edward Young, "This procedure is based upon a philosophical position that is essentially anti-metaphysical. It aims directly at the destruction of the historical basis of true Christianity."[255] Those who argue against the Bible, especially the New Testament view, know that the Gospel is grounded on the historical basis of Christianity in showing what God did for humanity. So if this historical basis goes, Christianity may as well go with it.

The Christian God is the creator of all things visible and invisible. The Spirit exists in utter independence of anything outside of Himself. He is an unchangeable, eternally infinite being, and He is utterly self-sufficient. As the prophets and the Gospel proclaimed, God reveals Himself through the spoken word and in the constitution of the created universe.

---

255   Edward J. Young, *My Servants the Prophets*, 191.

In light of the controversy concerning homosexuality and the source of the universe, the apostle Paul said,

> *The time will come when they will not endure sound doctrine, but according to their own desires, because they will have itching ears. They will heap up for themselves false teachers; and they will turn their ears away from the truth, and be turned aside to fables.*[256]

This age demonstrates the description by Paul; they prefer myths and endless genealogy and provoke controversies to excuse from God's path.[257]

Perception of God changes repeatedly between religious and geological standpoints. Different secular generations associate God with different ideas of earthly philosophy. This newest age has a mind-set that views every reality as virtual reality. Its perception of God recalls the plural viewpoint by Satan when he suggested to Adam and Eve in the Garden of Eden that by eating the forbidden fruit they would not die but be like God. Satan said,

> *Your eyes will be opened, and you will be like God, knowing good and evil.*[258]

Satan seems to imply that, by having opened eyes, people could be God; and if it were so, God would be no more. The concept is an old trick, which holds this generation captive. Many people perceive every theory as truth and disqualify the objective truth and its moral worth. We have lost the standard for measuring right and wrong ideas; every truth is assumed suspicious among a host of diverse

---

256   2 Tim. 4:3–4
257   1 Tim. 1:4
258   Gen. 3:5

communities. The satanic concept that there is no right and wrong deteriorates humanity's integrity and moves humanity away from the center of the universe. According to this generation, there is no center. The modern perspective locates everyone on a pyramid of fantasy and feeds on our feelings. The situation is a human tragedy; it greatly affects our marriage and family values. God initiated family as the cornerstone of any human development, but unlike any other generation in history, this generation is comfortable with paradox. Things can be and cannot be at the same time. Nothing is an exception; everything is admissible life, and everything is assumed possible to live with. As the complexity grows, the result is a society with a broken mental system. Today's tenet is a worldview that denies all worldviews—an age where the basic rule on how to live is to live with no rules. Many people favor negotiating the truth, but they forget that changing the truth will affect the fruit. Truth and moral value are relatives; they should not be seen as mere social constructs and a host of diverse communities.

A cure to this age's problem is to battle pluralism. We hold moral principles in the Bible to be absolute. Failure to differentiate between these principles and cultural assumptions will always lead to ambiguity. Belief is a unique function of any moral society; it is not part of assumptions that people make about themselves, the world around them, and ultimate realities. In the modern mentality revival without discipline could be harmful. The Gospel is not a part of many assumptions of life; it is the way to life. Things are not getting better, as complexity is allowed to widen.

Christians may take blame for proclaiming God's truth as the only saving truth, but compromising the truth is not a practical option. I am concerned that the confusion of belief among various groups will not settle unless theology, the root of the Christian belief, is clearly separated from the foothold of false beliefs. Advocates of religious tolerance are simply demanding that God change His nature.

*But if only for this life we have hope in Christ, we are to be
pitied more than all men."*[259]
*You confess with your mouth the Lord Jesus, and believe in
your heart that God has raised Him from the dead, you will be
saved. For with the heart one believes unto righteousness, and
with the mouth confession is made unto salvation.*[260]

Religion as an instrument of cultural perception relates to
people's opinion about God; it is a pursuit of ideas, not reality. Its
subject of discussion may, as is the case in some parts of the world,
even rule out the existence of God. Among the notions that add
to the plurality of approaches to God is the religious concept that
there are no wrong or right paths to God. Such concepts are found
in social, anthropological, and philosophical analyses of how people
view God. The idea is centered on a personal god—a collection
of supernatural beings and forces within nature that originates
according to an individual's preference for relating to God and
includes either sets of rituals, ethnic behaviors, or both.

By contrast, theology is not a part of the analysis. The theological
concept of God is different and definitive. Theology refers to the
study of God and His ways. The concept includes neither the god of
philosophers' viewpoints nor the viewpoints of any other religious
sect; rather it focuses solely on God in Christian context. Theological
study exercises the choice to seek true knowledge of God from the
Bible and its relatives.[261] Theology is the only discipline that strives
to give coherent statements of the doctrines of the Christian faith,
which is based primarily on the Bible. The Bible and theology are

---

259   1 Cor. 15:19
260   Rom. 10:9–10
261   "This book of the law shall not depart from your mouth, but you shall
       meditate on it day and night that you may observe to do according to
       all that is written in" (Josh. 1:8).

not only essential for human relationship with God; each serves as a gateway to correct doctrinal belief and practices:

That everyone may know how to posses his own vessel in sanctification and honor.[262]

Unlike theology, religion represents a general picture of reality, which shows how humanity is seeking God with its own ideas. From the shadow of religion, secular thoughts about God are formed. These thoughts are based on an understanding that every opinion matters and, therefore, we should not ignore any opinion. If different things should be God at different times and if God should represent all sorts of ideas and images, God is vague. Life's purpose must not continue to mean different things to different people. The only advantage of religion is that the concept keeps everyone busy believing in something.

Religion will not solve the problem of humanity's search for God; theology has. Divine revelation is the only source of theology throughout history, and despite how boring God's truth may seem to any generation it is the only saving truth. We read,

Let us seek the Lord while He may still be found, and call upon Him while He is still near. For His thoughts are not our thoughts and His ways are not our ways.[263]

---

262   1 Thess. 4:4

263   Isa. 55:6; "For as the heavens are higher than the earth, so are my ways higher than your ways; and my thoughts than your thoughts" (Isa. 55:8–9).

Chapter 4

⌐⋙∽

The Church and Church

The usefulness of Church to community indicates a blessing to be by showing that life is far greater than any personal fulfillment. The Sunday morning congregation is a fair measure of community's interest in God and concludes how we think of ourselves. If you recognize the need to attend Church worship, you may as well recognize the need to pray for all people. Searching for life's purpose outside godliness will leave us empty. There is no purpose to life except in God. Sunday morning worship is generally the Church's primary expression of itself in any given community.

As sufficient means of looking good when meeting with a familiar public, Christians worldwide wear pretty clothes when attending Sunday worship. Faithfully attended and properly conducted, Church worship represents an efficient but not sufficient way of accomplishing the central task of godliness. Pleasant outfit may literally reflect God's goodness to His people, but no one should be so carried away by the concept that he or she disregards the importance of purity of heart. Jesus confers to us a new model of humility by associating us to the Holy Spirit. The Christians' pleasant outfit should reflect on the outside the goodness that comes from within. Body and soul are partners in worship, which is connected to both conduct and appearance.

It is misleading to assume that one should reflect godliness only when he or she is in groups like those gathered for Sunday morning worship and prayer meetings. True goodness consists of one constantly embracing God with his or her entire self.

Goodness on the outer body alone is a double standard. Jesus named the practice of focusing solely on one's outer appearance "whitewashed grave."[264] The sense is that when one conceives worship internally in the goodness of God, it takes captive the entire self—reflected in inner thought, conduct, appearance, and utterance. Your dressy look will not be a sham if you are clean inside:

> You also like living stones are being built into a spiritual house
> to be a holy priesthood, offering spiritual sacrifices acceptable
> to God through Jesus Christ.[265]

Pride that Must Humble Us

The Holy Spirit is the key to godliness; He is the power that fulfills the law and frees us from the string of the law.

> Live by the Spirit, and you will not obey the evil desires of the
> flesh. For the flesh desires what is contrary to the Spirit, and the
> Spirit, what is contrary to the flesh. They are in conflict with
> each other, so that you do not do what you want. But if you are
> led by the Spirit, you are not under the law.[266]

---

264   Matt. 23:27; Acts 23:3
265   1 Peter 2:5, believers derive the life giving Spirit from Christ.
266   Gal. 5:16–18

The unrelenting conflict between the indwelling Holy Spirit and evil desires of the body cannot be resolved by human strength. The Spirit's power is an essential, reliable part of success against the struggle. Paul maintains that we are indebted to the Holy Spirit—that we must live according to His desire. We are bound to mistakes when we rely only on our natural intelligence. Living according to the flesh sharply contradicts the Holy Spirit's desire. Sinful desire stirs one's old self, but the Holy Spirit humbles one's attitude.

To take part in the winning process, you must humble yourself to the Holy Spirit's guidance. The process is self-transforming and can be regarded as being born again. The Holy Spirit gradually uplifts a person, helping him or her to be mindful that God watches over us.

Carnal mind is an enemy of God. Those who live by the flesh alone think only in the flesh; the outcome of their lifestyle does not often please God.[267]

Our lives are open before God; the awareness of His presence is a reason to honor Him. God's eyes are on the world in every moment; a humble heart knows this and struggles to put away all ungodliness. If we are reverent, God's nearness should regulate some of our actions and thought. Apparently all Christians receive the Holy Spirit when they first believe, but involvement with the Holy Spirit depends on personal openness to His desire. Despite anyone's claim to holiness, whoever does not live the experience of His indwelling presence is not fully christened.

Genuine Christians have the ability to allow the Holy Spirit to guide them toward what is characteristic of true believers. The apostle Paul rebaptized a group of believers in Ephesus so that they too received the Holy Spirit. Paul asked the believers,

267   Rom. 8:7–8

Did you receive the Holy Spirit when you believe? And they answered, "No, we have not even heard that there is a Holy Spirit." When Paul placed his hands on them, the Holy Spirit came on them, and they spoke in tongues and prophesied.[268]

From the early Church days, believers receive the Holy Spirit in a variety of ways. In this case, the signs signify the Holy Spirit's endorsement of the people as true believers. Prophesy and tongues are not the only obvious signs of the Holy Spirit.

No one can say "Jesus is Lord," except by the Spirit.[269]

The Ephesians believers were part of the Church, but their knowledge of the resurrected Christ was incomplete. They did not fully understand the significance of His death and the revival work of the Holy Spirit until soon after they received the Holy Spirit. The Ephesians' incident supports the case that the mark of a true Church is not merely right doctrine but also right action—the true evidence of the Holy Spirit.

To support His work, we ought to grow in humility and love, constantly putting to death any sin in our mind. Somehow, everyone is capable of making mistakes; to err has become part of human nature. Whenever you realize that you have made a mistake, accept the shame and the responsibility to make amends. Always reconcile your mistake also in prayer and overcome such behavior by changing your behaviors and moving toward goodness. Perfectionism is not an honor to Christianity, but it is better to err on the side of God's mercy than on the threshold of the devil. Admitting mistakes shows humility and reflects that you honor God.

---

268   Acts 19:2; Acts 19:6
269   1 Cor. 12:3

Your humble spirit should prompt you to review yourself first. On the contrary, obligating other people to behave properly will not bring you honor, especially when your lifestyle is not a testimony to true goodness.[270] It is easier to study God's laws and tell others to obey them than to set an example by practice.

The characteristics that bother us about other people are often the habits we dislike in ourselves, and it is likely that our untamed behavior patterns are often the very ones we most want to change in other people. I remember being in a Sunday morning worship organized by a Reformed Church in the South Province of Holland. While putting himself together to pray and therefore conclude the sermon, the minister said, "Brothers and sisters, I have not preached to you alone but also to myself, and God knows that it is true. For, I felt the power of His word redeeming me as I spoke."

I was pleased when I heard him. The holiness of God's word enabled the minister to see himself clearly as he was (which all of us are)—human beings who are unworthy of God's righteousness but can be redeemed through grace and the worthiness of the word. Such a view of ourselves helps us long daily for God and relates positively to our inner perception of the truth.

God resists the proud but gives grace to the humble. Therefore, humble yourself before the mighty God that He may exalt you in due time, casting all your care upon Him, for He cares for you.[271]

Another way you may look at humility with regard to worship is to consider yourself a servant of the Lord, rather than a member of His kingdom. Always present yourself to the Lord like a servant before his or her master. No one is better than anyone else; all

270   Matt. 7:3–4
271   1 Pet. 5:5–6

persons have an equal standing before God. The arrogant have an attitude that suggests they have no sin and, therefore, no real need of a Savior. An arrogant person can scorn; he or she lacks the spirit of humanity and the love of God. Jesus mocked people of such character, such as the Pharisees, to whom He said,

> *It is not the healthy who need a doctor but the sick. Go and learn what this means: I desire mercy, not sacrifice; for I have not come to call the righteous, but sinners.*[272]

Ironically, those who are sure of their safety do not need to be saved. Jesus implied the paradox to show that those who scorn bear shame. While the Pharisees questioned and debated Jesus, people were being healed and lives changed right in front of them, but they received no blessing.

> *No man can redeem the life of another or give to God a ransom for him. The ransom for a life is costly, no payments is ever enough that he should live on forever and not see decay. Man despite his riches does not endure; he is like the beasts that perish. This is the fate of those who trust in themselves, and of their followers, who approve of their sayings.*[273]

Scorn is the attitude of those who believe they have no need for God—those who see themselves either by their wealth as perfect or by their understanding of knowledge as all-knowing. They qualify themselves to all aspect of life's goodness and deny God's hand in their life. We should not forget that we have no hand in shaping our destiny. Basically, no amount of personal attribute can keep anyone from

---

272   Matt. 9:12–13
273   Ps. 49:7–9; Ps. 49:12–13

God's power.[274] Humble attitude is an important factor in order for a true heart of worship and bears more blessing than achievement.

Through Cain, we learn that God may reject one's prayer and thanksgiving because of one's attitude. To insist on false pride—denying sin and the equality of human beings, for example—is illusive. The habit accuses God of lying. His word declares universal sin, of which the entire world is guilty. Given the diverse use and the great benefit to spirituality, confession is a good remedy to the sin of pride. However, neither confession nor repentance allows us to escape certain consequences of wrongdoing. God does not guarantee that He will restore fellowship on the basis of confession alone, and God does not guarantee restoration of certain damages resulting from sin on the basis of either repentance or confession. Natural aftermath follows every sin. Nevertheless, true confession is a qualification that prepares the mind to receive God's blessing. If you ask, your sin will be erased in the blood of the Lord Jesus Christ.

Confession does not deny human weakness; believers are to use confession to seek God's redemption and normalize their relations with their neighbors. We read in James,

> *Therefore confess your sin to each other and pray for each other so that you may be healed. The prayer of a righteous person is powerful and effective.*[275]

You should concern yourself first with reuniting with your neighbor and then with uniting with God in prayer.

We cannot make all things right, at least not in this lifetime; but we can show honesty to God's presence and to the dwelling of saints.

---

274   "If we claim to be without sin we deceive ourselves and the truth is not in us; if we confess our sins, He is faithful and just and will forgive us our sins and cleanse us from all unrighteousness" (1 John 1:8–9).

275   James 5:16

Confession brings no relief when it does not carry the commitment to discontinue wrongdoing. God made a twofold provision as a measure of faith—His gracious love bestowed on His Son to restore holiness in all individual worship and the Holy Spirit's illumination, which helps to keep alive the servant attitude of Jesus Christ.

Jesus' life demonstrates that a true servant does not use his master's purpose for his own gain. Rather, a true servant simply carries out the master's purpose to the best of his or her ability and to the glory of the master. Jesus is our advocate and role model; His Spirit proceeds from the Father and pleads the case of unrepentant sinners, that all may finally repent and receive God's salvation.

Jesus' story exemplifies self-denial. His stewardship counts for the spiritual benefit of all people. His righteousness is so strong it can secure God's pardon for all. He asked God's forgiveness and suffered in exchange, not for Himself, but on behalf of all children of this world. God appointed Jesus Christ to appease sin and humbled Him to accept the task of His death.

> *There is no difference, for all have sinned and fall short of the glory of God, and are being justified freely by His grace through the redemption that came by Christ Jesus. God presented Him as a sacrifice of atonement, through faith in His blood. He did this to demonstrate His justice at the present time, so as to be just and the one who justifies those who have faith in Jesus.*[276]

In the Old Testament, we find records of people like Noah, Joshua, Caleb, Ruth, Hannah, and Samuel; God commends their obedience and humility of worship.[277] They stand before us as witnesses that the new covenant requirement on humility is attainable.

---

276   Rom. 3:23–26
277   Gen. 6:9; Num. 14:24

Pride is human ego at work; its version of self-esteem brings into play unwarranted class distinction and prejudice that exist in our society. Pride is driven by a secular viewpoint on gender, political and ethnic differences, and unbalanced social and economic ranks. Such vision of inequality has no place in communal fellowship of saints. Christian pride is not a result of personal beauty and fulfillment but of the oneness of God working in all people:

> *Let him who boasts boast about this: that he understands and knows me, that I am the Lord who exercises kindness, justice, and righteousness on Earth, for in these I delight.*[278]

To prioritize delightful worship in one's life is to reflect love and justice. If you glorify yourself, your glory is nothing. Those who claim importance could add nothing to God; and whatever they are makes no difference to His power. The characteristic damage of self-importance is like a black spot on the heart of the Church. Pride is essentially the cause of segregation. Those who gather from negative emotion use the emotion to promote segregation. Money is not the only source of pride; people are arrogant about their opportunities. If we think thoughtfully, we will realize that wealth, which includes opportunity and talent, is God given. Worshipping Him is the sole purpose of life, and all that we benefit from we have received in His name.[279] God dignifies humanity by giving humanity exceptional qualities. You are unique in whatever way that you are gifted, and you are required to uniquely employ your gifts to the glory of God.

In his first letter to the Church of Corinth, the apostle Paul metaphorically compares the Church to a human body, demonstrating

278   Jer. 9:24; 1 Cor. 1:31
279   Ps. 23

how diverse talent could naturally assure progress in the Church. Every talent contributes some worth that is necessary and beneficial to the common life of the Church.

Life in the Spirit provides no room for self-esteem and inferiority complex. Despite the little that you may be gifted, you are part of the body and essential to the proper functioning of the body. If you do not realize and strive for this truth, laziness may give way to failure, which may result in hatred for the Master. Whoever claims that he or she does not have enough and, therefore, should not work to glorify God risks forfeiting whatever he or she has. And whoever exalts him or herself will be humbled.[280]

The basic unity within diverse gift is of no other source than the Holy Spirit. By Him:

The greatest among you should be your servant.[281]

The gift of the Holy Spirit is the common life of the Church and a greater dynamic than all human distinction.

As the body is one and has many parts, but all the parts are of that one body, being many, are one body, so also is Christ. For by one Spirit we were all baptized into one body.[282]

All true believers are priests and should encourage each other to practice faithful worship. Praying for one another is important. Your prayer should support people's efforts to overcome such weaknesses as pride. The entire body of the Church struggles against many weaknesses, and therefore, we must work together to keep on winning the fight.

---

280   Matt. 23:12; Matt. 25:14–30 – the Parable of the Talents
281   Matt. 23:11
282   1 Cor. 12:12–13

A person's life is worth more than an abundance of possessions. The poor should not feel intimidated for not possessing as much as the rich. Job said,

> *If I have put my trust in gold or said to pure gold "You are my security." If I have rejoiced over my great wealth, the fortune my hands had gained. If I have regarded the sun in its radiance or the moon moving in splendor, so that my heart was secretly enticed and my hand offered them a kiss of homage. Then these also would be sins to be judged, for I would have been unfaithful to God on high.*[283]

Selflessness is another good cure for the problem of pride. Job implies selflessness as having the receptiveness that constitutes humility. To be receptive is to have a recipient ear to the voice of the Spirit. We can expect decay when we value anything more than God. By staying in touch with the Holy Spirit, we will have the wisdom to meet life's great challenges. When we overcome problems like pride, as was the case with Job's three friends, the experiences we've lived become great teachers and testimonies of hope.[284]

According to the psalmist, each day is an experience that teaches us to number rightfully the rest of days.[285] Our desires can only be satisfied in eternity; presently, we must apply ourselves to survive the earthly struggle.

Let us bear in mind the parable of the Pharisee and the tax collector. The parable is told to counsel people whose self-importance has constituted self-righteousness. Under the siege of Rome, Jews

---

283   Job 31:24–28
284   Job 42:7–10; Job's friends made the error of assuming that Job's suffering was caused by some great sin. They judged with arrogance without knowing what God was doing.
285   Ps. 90:11–12

viewed indigenous tax collectors as traitors for extorting citizen's money on behalf of the imperial administration of the Roman Empire. With the emergence of such a critical political and religious atmosphere, Jesus told the people this parable:

Two men went into the temple to pray, one a Pharisee and the other a tax collector. The Pharisee stood and prayed about himself, "God, I thank you that I am not like other men; robbers, evil doer, adulterers, or even like this tax collector. I fast twice a week and I give tithes of all that I possess." But the tax collector stood at a distance. He would not even raise his eyes to heaven but beat his chest, saying, "God, be merciful to me, a sinner."[286]

The tax collector's prayer indicates sincere recognition of guilt and willingness to learn from God; whereas the Pharisee prayed about his self-worth. Humility is like a debt; we owe it to God and our neighbors. Jesus ended the parable by saying,

The tax collector went back to his house justified rather than the Pharisee. For everyone who exalt himself will be humbled, and he who humble himself will be exalted.[287]

The parable corrects the notion that righteousness can be a human achievement. It demonstrates how religion that is built upon a system of merit is likely to lead to pride and, therefore, to hypocrisy.

Pharisee in biblical idiomatic expression is almost an alternative word to self-importance, hypocrisy, and self-righteousness. We dare

---

286   Luke 18:9–13
287   Luke 18:14

not bear self-righteousness in our attitude toward God, thinking that God will feel honored, while we humiliate fellow worshippers.

Blessed are the meek, for they shall inherit the earth; and blessed are those who hunger and thirst for righteousness, for they shall be filled.[288]

The way to God's kingdom is by faith, which means the experience of hope and joy, free from outward circumstances.

Prayer House, Not Theatre

Prayer is not a show of faith. The grand motivation to pray should be desire for God's approval and fear of His disapproval. Exercising prayer is spiritualizing; prayer is an uttermost outburst of the inner mind. God's house is no theatre; it is a sanctuary—a place of special meeting with His presence.

Perversion of the uses of God's house frustrate peoples' attempt at worship. If we commercialize God's house, we are dedicating the sacred building to unholy purpose. The amount of money invested in building and beautifying a place of worship should not be the judge of its worth. A beautiful house of worship does not always guarantee heartfelt worship of God. Providing opportunity to true worship does not ensure that true worship will be realized.

Efforts to build and maintain a place of worship must be guided by the power of the Spirit that is at work in God's people; in other words, the beauty of a place of worship should reflect the inner personality of those who build and maintain it, not the virtue of the architecture. Competence and decency constitute honor, but competent and decent construction does not guarantee the fullness of the Spirit's presence in Church.

288   Matt. 5:5–6

When God's people gather, who is who in regard to appearance should play no psychological role; rather, the focus should be on the Holy Spirit. Believers achieve the aim of gathering before God's presence by setting the tone in oneness of faith. One's appearance may partly reveal one's state of mind, and sometimes it can suggest one's personality, but appearance alone does not necessarily reveal one's spiritual standing. A gentle appearance constitutes humility, but humility is not about appearance. In the name of honor, Christians must rise to the challenge and put a better face on the psychology of our worship habits. We should moderate the dress we wear to attend Church in order to appear gentle, and we should focus more on the sacred attraction of God's house.

God is good to His people; therefore, God's people ought to testify to His goodness in all aspects of worship. Worship is the act of being nice to God and in the name of God to all people. Jesus appeared meek during His days, while on earth He accommodated Himself within the social and economic standing of His time. Jesus did not outweigh His followers and the people around Him, even though He lacked nothing.

With regard to fashion, certain outfits serve only self-attraction; the form does not constitute any of the believers' priorities. Unnecessary self-attraction can sometimes bring mistrust between pastors and their congregation. Without a doubt, some pastors outweigh their congregation. I was part of a Church in which members, who for the most part lived in poverty, were heavily taxed so that the leadership could have more comfortable lives. I've heard of Christians who withdrew their membership from a Church because they felt they didn't have the quality clothes and expensive cars to match the competition. The believers developed self-pity by watching their leaders place emphasis on material gain; accordingly, they withdrew from the Church.

The Church's gathering should not resemble a fashion show; nor should it be a heavy tax burden to anyone. Like the apostles said, donation should be voluntary, appropriate, and systematic. Particularly with fashion, overdressing and underdressing are, predictably, dangerous psychological ploys by which Satan can take advantage of mindless Christians. A simple and clean outfit is ideal for public gatherings like Church worship. If all worshippers adhered to this guideline, believers would more easily see themselves as reasonably equal.

Certain occasions may demand the use of expensive and culturally appropriate attire. It is not wrong to acquiesce to the demand, especially if you can genuinely afford the outfit. Assure yourself that such an outfit and makeup does, by no means, rule over you.

It is advisable that, during worship gatherings, you appear only in attire that will help you humble yourself before God. Expensive clothes, jewelry, and heavy makeup could psychologically isolate you amid fellow worshippers, in the same way that tattered dress and queer fashion could make you look irresponsible. The people around you could interpret your tattered outfit as mindlessness and, therefore, deny you their respect. You could seem to be suggesting that God is not treating you well and you have nothing in Him to celebrate.

Analysis concludes that neat, gentle attire will enable us to humble ourselves in the presence of the Almighty God. As it is said, cleanliness is next to godliness. On the other hand, those who dress to appear rich and famous determine their value as a person by worldly standards. Somehow the attitude is sinful and the concept is immoral. By discriminating, we reveal evil thought such as pride and covetousness. The apostle James said,

My brothers, as believers in our glorious Lord Jesus Christ, don't show favoritism. Suppose a man comes into your meeting wearing a gold ring and fine clothes, and a poor man in shabby

clothes also comes in. If you show special attention to the man wearing fine clothes, and say, "Here is a good seat for you," but say to the poor man, "You stand there" or "Sit on the floor by my feet," have you not discriminated among yourselves and become judge with evil thoughts?[289]

No one may hold onto faith on the basis of discrimination and self-glory. No one lives unto himself, and no one dies to himself; whatever each person is and does effects the others. Outward looks can be illusive—they can deny the goodness of someone's or fail to show all that a person is. Wealth is not measured by money alone. Wealth can be tallied in terms of intelligence, good health, high spiritual standing, peace of mind, and ability to do hard work.

Wealth can also be evidence of greed, selfishness, and dishonesty. Two of rich people's barriers to salvation are pride and power. The poor are usually sensitive to their powerlessness; the things they lack often draw them to easily accept God's salvation.

Poverty is no qualification to entrance into heaven, and wealth is no gateway to hell. Everyone who is faithful in this life has untold riches in heaven. Unfortunately, desire for riches and regard to appearance adds to the problem of segregation, which should not influence the Church.

Based on modern outlook on appearance, fatal fancy has emerged as pride's counterpart. The pinnacles of fatal fancy include body tattooing, cosmetic surgery like breast implants and face lifts, and sex reassignment therapy. The Lord said,

Do not cut your bodies for the dead or put tattoo marks on yourselves.[290]

---

289   James 2:1–4
290   Lev. 19:28

We should not disfigure our bodies after the manner of pagans. Such laceration and disfigurement were common among early pagans as a sign of mourning or a mark of beautification to secure the attention of their deity. It is unfortunate that some Christians partake in such negative attitudes against the body. Imagine the damage to natural beauty and spiritual sanctity. Sanctity of body and soul is essential in this life as worship is to the hereafter.

The usefulness of body and soul in the afterlife is the reason that Isaiah said,

But your dead will live; their bodies will rise"[291]

If the dead will be raised imperishable and the mortal made immortal, how will the surgically redesigned present themselves to the Lord on the day of His coming? They may have no share in the transformation of the saints, having surgically recreated themselves, an indication that God lacked the skill to make them perfect.

This materially motivated attitude may gain the world's favor but certainly not God's. Cosmetic surgery is a practical joke by the evil one—through the idea that cosmetic surgery is necessary, Satan lures men and women to believe that God is not dependable. Jesus said,

Whoever desires to come after me, let him deny himself, and take up his cross, and follow me. For whoever desires to save his life will lose it, but whoever loses his life for my sake, and for the Gospel's sake will save it. What will it profit a man if he gains the whole world, yet forfeit his soul? Or what can a man give in exchange for his soul? If anyone is ashamed of me and my words in this adulterous and sinful generation, the Son of

---

291   Isa. 26:19

man will be ashamed of him when He comes in His Father's
glory with the holy angels.[292]

The concern is not merely the high cost of discipleship; God
tests our relationship with Him to ascertain whether it is our highest
priority. The Lord Jesus knows the difficulty of an earthly life and
asks that we let Him guide us. Fatal fancy and the consciousness
that it creates has turned certain stations in life, such as old age, into
something negative, rather than a blessing of God. It is currently
offensive to refer to a person as aged. Whereas age-conscious people
desire to look young, they dare to ask for respect suitable to their
natural age. The Church should not treat the secular notion of age
as mere worldview and social maxim. Age rejection constitutes an
anti-God view. No physician can guarantee old age; God gives
abundance of life as special favor.

Faith that comes from true knowledge of God is not some
passive response of shallow-minded Christians. A true faith does
not waiver. Old age is one of the greatest blessings of God; those
who receive the opportunity to grow old should consider themselves
lucky for being so kindly honored. No money can afford old age.
People of all ages—rich and poor alike—suffer untimely deaths. To
live through many years is a rare opportunity of grace. Gray hair is
an honor; the head should wear it like a crown.

Methuselah, Abraham, Enoch, Job, David, and Simeon[293] are
among the favored few in the Bible. These men experienced real
old age before they died, and they were grateful to God.[294] It is
better to die in good, old age than to die young. Regret about aging
is humanity's ingratitude toward the graciousness of God. Fatal
fancy is already part of the Western mental culture; it is gaining

---

292   Mark 8:34–38
293   Luke 2:25–33
294   Job 42:17

momentum in the rest of the world. Unbelievers take pleasure in living big and in dressing rich; they like to appear young and sexy as a means of feeling socially attractive and acceptable. The fear that cultivates fatal fancy in peoples' minds captivates them to insist on outward adornment. Many people are willing to do whatever it may cost to remain noticeably young and sexually attractive. To these many, being sexy, rich, and famous is better than being righteous.

However, the luxury of riches is no stain to godliness if one is genuinely blessed. As we read in 1 Chronicles,

Both riches and honor comes from God. He reigns over all.[295]

Jesus never stood against material wealth and enjoyment derived from material things of life. He enjoyed the hospitality of many rich people; the Pharisees called Him names like food lover, wine bibber, and friend of sinners.[296]

Jesus is against selfish and extravagant attitude of materialism, which ties a person to this world. He said,

But seek you first His kingdom and His righteousness, and all these things will be given to you as well.[297]

It is better to seek the blessing of God than to get in trouble with earthly riches. A godless society is hostile to God's kingdom and therefore to God's plan.

It takes wisdom to survive in a nonbelieving world, in a setting that is, for the most part, hostile to true faith. We can demonstrate wisdom by showing our respect for the truth. Christians should

---

295   1 Chron. 29:12
296   Luke 7:33–34
297   Matt. 6:33

observe proper modesty, free from worldly dross. The apostle Paul said to Timothy,

> *Command those who are rich in this present age not to be haughty, nor to trust in uncertain riches but in the living God who gives us richly all things to enjoy.*[298]

A Christian way to be socially attractive is by exhibiting fear of God, empathy, moral behavior, self-respect, and hard work. There is no hint of merit here on Earth; therefore, being socially attractive demands that Christians be kind, especially to strangers:

> *Even when we are continuing with our brotherly and sisterly love, we should not forget to entertain strangers that are in our midst. For by so doing, some people have unknowingly entertained angels.*[299] *Blessed is the man who walks not in the path of the ungodly, nor stands in the path of sinners, nor sits in the seat of the scornful but his delight is in the law of the Lord.*[300]

Delightful worship does not require the sexy look and attitude of our modern society. God does not require His children to think and appear worldly.[301] Ours is to look modest:

> *Your beauty should not come from outward adornment, such as braided hair and the wearing of gold and jewelry and fine clothes. Instead, it should be that of your inner self, the unfading beauty of a gentle and quite spirit, which is of worth in God's sight.*[302]

---

298   1 Tim. 6:17
299   Heb. 13:1–2
300   Ps. 1:1–2
301   Isa. 3:16–26
302   1 Peter 3:3–4

No house of worship is a business center, and none should be looked upon or managed as such. The house of worship is a spiritual hospital. In the book, *Intimacy with God*, I discussed in greater detail than I have here the concept of the house of worship as a spiritual hospital, capturing every kind of spiritual sickness as curable through the wondrous word of God.

You will distract fellow worshippers if you choose to appear sexy in any of the Church's gathering. The least distraction could easily mislead the vulnerable. The Church has plenty of people who are easily detached by wrong example as a result of personal weakness. The punishment for misleading any of God's children is severe. It is better to drown than to cause a saved soul to backslide and fall.[303]

No sin exists in a vacuum; every sinful act will likely affect someone else, and likewise, living the right way will affect others. This generation predominantly suffers mental and spiritual corruption, which unfiltered television program and Internet surfing without caution brings. The word of God is always the Spirit force by people's lives change and our common behavior improves.

We should not be deterred by the claim that only people of failed life seek God's help. Satan blocks the brain and the eyes of our accusers; they neither realize the danger of hellfire nor perceive the reality, which the Gospel holds for repentant soul. Those who accept God's salvation shall glory in the Lord; by His grace those few are saved through faith.[304] The saved are channels of spiritual

---

303   "Things that cause people to sin are bound to come, but woe to that person through whom they come. It would be better for him to be thrown into the sea with a millstone tied around his neck than for him to cause one of these little ones to sin. So, watch yourselves" (Luke 17:1–3).

304   "Those who are well have no need for a physician, but those who are sick. I have not come to call the righteous, but sinners to repentance" (Luke 5:31–32).

blessing to people in darkness; without the promise of God even faith will save no one:

> *It is not through Law that Abraham and his offspring receive the promise that he would be heir of the world, but through the righteousness that comes by faith. For, if those who live by Law are heirs, faith has no value and the promise is worthless.*[305]

Jesus said,

> *He who believes in me, out of his heart will flow rivers of living water.*[306]

Prayer Model and the Tradition

The kingdom of heaven came to Earth when God entered human history as a man—first as a suffering servant for the sins of the world and then by the Spirit as victorious conqueror of sin and death. The kingdom of heaven will not be fully realized until Jesus' Second Coming, when evil in the world will be judged and come to an end.

Jesus continues to offer Himself as the cornerstone of the new kingdom. He reigns in the heart of His believers. Scripture foretold the role Jewish people played in accomplishing the task of Jesus' death:

> *The stone the builders rejected has become the cornerstone.*[307]

Because many Jews, especially the Pharisees, rejected Jesus, Gentiles were qualified to accept the Gospel. According to Simeon when he held the child Jesus in the temple,

---

305   Rom. 4:13–14

306   John 7:38

307   Ps. 118:22; Matt. 21:42

Behold, this child is destined to cause the falling and rising of many in Israel, and to be a sign that will be spoken against, so that the thoughts of many hearts will be revealed.[308]

The image of "the stone the builders rejected" shows how one truth can affect all people in different ways. The Jews were familiar with the prophecies that spoke of the Messiah's blessing on their nation, but they did not always give the same attention to the prophecies that would bring salvation to the entire world.

In chapter 49, Isaiah told the people what the Lord meant with the new kingdom of His worshippers:

It is too small a thing for you to be my servant to restore the tribes of Jacob and bring back those of Israel I have kept. I will also make you a light for the Gentiles, that you may bring my salvation to the end of the earth.[309]

The Pharisees, as well as many orthodox Jews, missed the point about the kingdom; as descendants of Abraham, they thought that they knew the mind of God better.[310]

As we know, the Bible tells us of John the Baptist preaching before it addresses Jesus' ministry. John introduced the message of repentance and the good news of Jesus' coming. By preaching relentless prayer and fasting, John reinvented Jewish prayer habit. Israel was accustomed to praying three times—morning, noon, and evening—but John exercised prayer in different way.[311]John began

---

308   The prophecy of Simeon – Luke 2:25–35; Luke 2:34–35

309   Isa. 49:6

310   "They answered Him, 'We are Abraham's descendants and have never been slaves to anyone. How can you say that we shall be set free?'" (John 8:33).

311   Ps. 55:17; Dan. 6:10

his ministry of baptism and repentance by spending time in the wilderness of Judea, praying and fasting. He clothed himself with camel's skin and ate locusts and wild honey.[312]

John's attitude toward prayer was no match for the tradition the people knew. For four hundred years before John, the nation of Israel lived without a true prophet in their midst. The people were amazed by the spiritual power of John's ministry, and the influence prompted the Pharisees to investigate John's authority. John practically lived the word he preached and, thereby, inspired the entire land. John's prayer habit made the Pharisees look like strangers to religiosity. As a result, they perceived John as acting differently and strongly criticized him among themselves. The Pharisees answered John by claiming that "he has a demon."[313]

But John continued to fascinate his Jewish audience in many wondrous ways. His preaching and water baptisms overwhelmingly appeased some of these religious leaders, and they sent priests from Jerusalem to ask John whether he was the Messiah.[314] A majority of the people believed in John's message and came forth to be baptized. Israel at the time was anticipating the coming of the Messiah, and many among the people looked upon John as either the prophet[315] foretold by Moses, who could be Elijah,[316] or the Messiah himself.

Isaiah prophesied about John's coming, referring to him as the Baptist. Isaiah foretold that John would play a role in the coming of Christ, saying John would be the forerunner,—

---

312   Matt. 3:1; Matt. 3:4

313   Luke 7: 33

314   John 1:19–22

315   "The Lord your God will raise up for you a prophet like me from among your own brothers. You must listen to him" (Deut. 18:15).

316   "See; I will send you the prophet Elijah before that great and dreadful day of the Lord comes" (Mal. 4:5).

The voice of one crying out from the wilderness.[317]

John prepared the way for the Messiah's coming by calling on the people to repent and be baptized. He prepared the peoples' mind like a king's representative would make advance preparation for the king's visit to a province of His realm.

Isaiah described John's baptism as

Smoothening and leveling of His paths; the making straight in the desert a highway for the Lord.[318]

The urgency of John's message is the nearness of God, which we cannot associate with sin and unbelief.

In a complementary way, John and the Pharisees shared the task of preparing the people to accept God's goodness. John was spiritually devoted to his message of repentance and to baptizing the people, while the Pharisees taught the people the usefulness of the laws of salvation. John recognized the importance of fasting and prayed for his task to be successful. John reached out for extra empowerment and received the spiritual assistance he needed. John did not preach only repentance; he fasted and prayed that the people be touched by the preached word.

When addressing the concept of worship, John put much emphasis on not sinning; he preached that nothing except sin could stop anyone from receiving God's salvation. In contrast, the Pharisees deceived themselves and the people they guided with hypocrisy. They both mocked God with their false beliefs and took advantage of the law to glorify themselves.

---

317   Isa. 40:3–5

318   Isa. 40:4; "Every valley shall be raised up, every mountain and hill made low; the rough ground shall become level; the rugged places plain. And the glory of the Lord will be revealed" (Isa. 49:11–13).

The healing power in John's message was, in part, the sign of God's deliverance to the people. Those touched by the power were made to acknowledge the truthfulness of the Lord Almighty. Stubbornly corrupt, a majority of the Pharisees did not recognize John as a prophet—not even after seeing the result of John's immense good work.[319]

John did not play the Messiah's role, but humbly he bore witness to the truth. John said,

> *I do not know Him, the Messiah, but He who sent me to baptize with water said to me, "Upon whom you see the Spirit descending and remaining on Him, this is He who baptizes with the Holy Spirit."*[320]

John maintained himself within the spiritual framework of his calling by not claiming power and position that were not his. We know that John's testimony is reliable and came from divine revelation. Scripture testifies of his message as true:

> *But more than that, blessed are those who hear the word of God and keep it.*[321]

The following are some conclusions drawn from John's prayer attitude. First, his attitude toward prayer is not in neglect of the

---

319   "The baptism of John—was it from heaven or from men?" (Jesus asked the Pharisees who questioned His authority) "They reasoned among themselves, saying, 'If we say, "From heaven," He will say, "Why then didn't you believe him?" But if we say, "From men," all the people will stone us, for they are persuaded that John was a prophet.' So they answered that they do not know where it came from" (Luke 20:4–7).

320   John 1:32–34

321   Luke 11:28

tradition, but for a better result. John reached out to the people because of his desperate love for them and his desire that they be saved. He performed the best that he could in order that the glory of God's promise be restored on Israel. John's sacrifice was a privilege that granted to the people, as his devotion pleased God, who called him to serve.

From the Gospel comes a similar privilege of intimacy. Believers, through prayer, share close friendship with God. In heartfelt prayer is spiritual kinship that manifests in one's ability to accomplish life's true purpose. On the other hand, daily recitation of prayers written in a common prayer book does little to help worshippers realize the relationship they could achieved through talking to God with personal thoughts and heartfelt words.

I do not mean to discredit the value of our common prayer and liturgy; these are useful, in the same way that catechisms allow us to recite our beliefs. I suggest that we offer also personal prayers that do not reflect the restrained nature of common prayers and, instead, include personal thoughts. The monotony of common prayer and liturgy kills the interest of worshippers who truly thirst for spiritual revival. Revival should not focus only on the method of administering prayer and liturgy but also on the attitude of the administrator.

As Anglicans ordained, I live the experience that could explain why written prayers are not sufficient to obtain a delightful, worshipful relationship with God or to build up good knowledge of biblical incidents. Good Bible knowledge makes possible the faith to live according to the lessons of the narrative. The task of every Christian is to discover how to recap the Bible incidents in prayer so as to gain intimacy with God. The true purpose of prayer is spiritual growth and a lifetime of true intimacy with God.

Recent investigations into why fewer youth are participating in traditional Churches suggest that prayer and liturgy are somehow boring to many youth. According to some of the youth, the habit does not warrant going to Church every Sunday. Further investigation about declining spirituality suggests that more youth are likely to reject prayer and worship, especially those brought up in traditional Christian homes.

The Bible contains numerous personal life stories showing difficult times. These stories invite the reader to see today's world as including similar experiences as a result of sin and unbelief, while understanding that closeness to God's word is the only solution to humanity's unhappiness. Nothing should replace the actual use of biblical narrative in building up moral society. The power of stories to change lives is illustrated by television and movies viewed around the world. It is no surprise that three out of every five pages of the Bible record the history of actual people and events. Biblical stories can influence readers' mind-sets, as every reader is supposed to identify him or herself in the events.

Biblical narrative provides a meditative, hands-on reality to devotion, which a list of laws and principles could never match. Even simpler narratives that are not fully developed in the Bible give faith roots in fact. The historical foundation of biblical truth safeguards against the mystical error of removing faith from daily life. Praying in biblical speech is a safeguard against the threat of the anti-supernaturalist, who degrades biblical faith in order to make it a belief without miracles.

The Bible is not bound to any change, but human nature, like tradition, mentality, and ideology, may continue to transform. Every believer should pray heartfelt words and personal experience frequently; doing so would aid personal vindication more than reciting a collection of prayers.

Certain occasion will always require the use of liturgical prayers, but we must modify with the times by improving our approach to God. My concern is that, in a season where prescribed prayers are the only form of prayer that some of the Christian public know, many people are neglecting the usefulness of prayer. Concerned Christians simply do not know how else to communicate their needs to God except by reciting the prayer book, which definitely isn't enough. As is the case with the Lord's Prayer, composed prayers are meant as guides, or rather the basic teachings of prayer, which should expand our thought to prayerfully accommodating our personal needs. Prayer ought to be mostly in one's words and thoughts—a heartfelt need and thanksgiving expressed through reference to biblical incidents.

My investigation on the subject further revealed that youth who are brought up in traditional homes easily learn the prayers in the book by heart, but only a few take to heart the true meaning of prayer and its spiritual demand. Some of the people in the discussion expressed how the habit of reciting prayers made them feel dull. They felt relieved when they finally left their parents' home. To them, the bullying finally ended; they now owed their lives to themselves. To these youth, saying good-bye to the God of their parents felt like a relief, as prayer seemed to be a punishment; people are not taught to open their mind to God in prayer using heartfelt statements.

The Bible is the authority that backs up your claim in prayer. John the Baptist did not keep his prayer habit to himself; he taught his disciples to pray. John believed in the importance of self-made prayer, and he prayed in own words to the finish line.

John the Baptist was not a better prayer warrior than Jesus Christ. Jesus' preaching and works of miracle drew to Him more of a crowd than John had. John kept himself in Judea, but Jesus traveled around. However, one should not compare John to Jesus by examining their respective prayers; their missions and personalities were different. John confessed that, after him, an authority mightier than he was would come. Referring to Jesus, John said,

My baptism to you is the baptism of water unto repentance, but when He comes, He will baptize you with Holy Ghost and fire.[322]

John administered the sign, which the Messiah bestowed. John's baptism offered the salvation experience of being baptized in the Holy Spirit. As John's baptism placed the people in the medium of water, so the baptism of Jesus Christ places Christians in the Spirit. Like John, Jesus is not against the prayer tradition. He said:

Anyone who breaks one of the least of these commandments, and teaches others to do the same, will be called least in the kingdom of heaven; but whoever practices and teaches these commands will be called great in the kingdom of heaven.[323]

Nevertheless, Jesus prayed even harder and longer with personal thoughts. Large crowds followed Jesus; among them were people who pressed on for His favor. Jesus made different prayers plan than those that John the Baptist embraced. On several occasions, Jesus withdrew himself from the crowd to a quiet place in order to have more time to pray. He did not count the hours, and He did not let anyone know where He was and what He had gone to do.[324] Jesus sparked the peoples' messianic passion; they wanted to install Him king by force—to make Him their political messiah.[325]

It is no surprise that the Pharisees did not notice Jesus praying as often as they noticed John the Baptist praying. The Pharisees criticized Jesus mostly about healing the sick on a Sabbath and eating in the house of tax collectors, who they regarded as sinners and traitors. Occasionally, they accused Jesus' disciples of doing things

---

322   Matt. 3:11
323   Matt. 5:19
324   John 6:15
325   John 6:15

like eating with unwashed hands, which the Pharisees considered unlawful according to Mosaic Law.[326] Furthermore, Jesus stepped out of the tradition in many other ways, as it was necessary for Him to attend to people in dire need of God's mercy.

Many of the Pharisees hated both Jesus and John, though they were never consistent in their faultfinding. One day, Jesus got upset and rebuked the Pharisees for their hypocrisy. The Pharisees accused Jesus of not praying hard like John the Baptist did; they murmured greatly against Jesus' claim that He is the Son of God. Jesus said to them,

John the Baptist came, neither eating bread nor drinking wine, and you say "He has a demon." The Son of man has come, eating and drinking and you say, "Look, a glutton and a wine bibber; a friends of tax collectors and sinners?"[327]

The Pharisees saw in both John the Baptist and Jesus Christ evidence of good worship, but they did not approve of either of them. They neither recognized Jesus Christ as the Messiah nor John the Baptist as a prophet. Neither John nor Jesus provided the political emphasis the Pharisees wanted in prayer and worship. The Pharisees' real objection to both men had nothing to do with prayer and dietary habits; the Pharisees and teachers of the law could not stand having their hypocrisy exposed.

Despite the accusations and the betrayal, Jesus prayed for the Jews, as He prays for all sinners—that all may repent and be forgiven by God. Jesus prayed on the cross,

Father, forgive them for they do not know what they do.[328]

---

326 "Then some of the pharisees and teachers of the law came to Jesus from Jerusalem and asked, 'Why do your disciples break the tradition of the elders? They don't wash their hands before they eat!'" (Matt. 15:1–2).

327 Luke 7:33

328 Luke 23:34

God answered Jesus' prayer by opening the way of salvation to also His murderers. Many of the Pharisees and Roman soldiers who witnessed how Jesus died on the cross believed in Him as truly the Son of God.[329]

The concept of Christ is reconciliation—the chance of a new beginning. His commitment speaks for the opportunity before us. Jesus is the cornerstone of forgiveness, to which John the Baptist dedicated his fasting and prayer. Jesus' passion in reconciling the world to God gives you the authority to help save souls. One is not bound to accept God's salvation if one does not truly understand its benefits. To teach God's salvation to the world is not a matter of tradition but a concern of love that involves the kingdom of God. Our response is intended to defend the truth about what Jesus Christ did to provide atonement for sin.

Like John, Prophet Jeremiah took actions before the Babylonian exile that showed how much he loved his people. Jeremiah did the best that he could to prevent Israel and Judah from captivity, although the sins of the people prevailed.[330] Jeremiah was persecuted for his truthfulness, but his compassionate love shows him to be righteous.

Those who are reconciled to Jesus Christ are commissioned to advance His message of hope. The Lord said,

The people to whom I am sending you are adamant and stubborn. Tell to them what I the sovereign Lord says, whether they listen or fail to listen.[331]

---

329   Matt. 27:54

330   "O my soul, my soul! I am pained in my very heart! My heart makes a noise in me; I cannot hold my peace because you have heard, o my soul, the sound of the trumpet, the alarm of war. Destruction is cried, for the whole land is plundered" (Jer. 4:19–21).

331   Ezek. 2:4–5

Now is not the time to hold the world against its stubbornness; people will realize the truth if we sufficiently persist in telling them its benefits.

The Lord's Prayer

The Lord's Prayer is a figurative representation of the Ten Commandments. Four of the commandments guide our attitude toward God, while six bring everyone together.

Jesus taught His disciples to pray primarily because they felt the need to pray, in a similar way that John the Baptist taught his disciples to pray.[332] Since the teaching of the Lord's Prayer, some believers simply recite the prayer, while others make it part of their daily prayer package.

The Lord's Prayer is part of the New Testament Bible and a model of prayer. The legitimacy of the prayer is the word of God. Jesus instructed His followers to say the prayer on a daily basis; He did not intend to suggest that this should constitute an unbendable ritual. The Lord's Prayer provides the characteristics of a good prayer to guide the conduct of our prayer. If you learn the Lord's Prayer with that purpose in mind, you will develop daily a new variety of prayer subjects and the desire to pray more.

The idea is to make your prayer reflect God's interest, your interests, and the interest of all people. It is important that you take into consideration the platform on which the Lord's Prayer is set when restructuring the subjects to suit your prayer needs. The term "Our Father" praises God as the father of humanity and obligates you to reflect in your prayer the need for all people to come under God's saving grace. This terminology implicates everyone's connection to God, the Father—God is our Father, our maker, and creator of the universe. The awareness of a universal

---

332   Luke 11:1–4; Matt. 6:9–13

God highlights the need to always begin prayer with praise and thanksgiving.

Prayer is neither a shopping list of needs and desires nor a forum for an appeal court. When you pray, "Hallowed be thy name. Thy will be done on Earth as it is done in heaven," remind yourself of the need to ask God to render his holiness present upon the earth, allowing the Holy Spirit to touch every soul, especially those seriously lost in sin. To share in God's holiness is to enjoy life in His presence and to be transformed into His likeness. The goal of such prayer is not simply absorption into the being of God, but also the transformation of the world for the glory of God.

When you pray, "Give us this day our daily bread," recall that everything you own is not practically yours. You are expected to help fulfill the day's ration for those who are deprived whenever you realize that there is more in your food store than you need. The surplus shows God's hand providing for you and through you for people in need. We desire God's blessed vision, and even more, we desire to bring our will and the will of all people into agreement with God's purpose.

God's provision is daily and sufficiently wondrous. You should not store up wealth in order to cut off communication with God. It is not necessary to have riches in order to practice giving; and your generosity must not be in the company that can afford your means. God teaches, through His only Son, Jesus Christ's example, that we must give willfully and from everything that we can afford.

Providing for the poor does not mean that we should share either less meaningful things or ration that which we would otherwise throw away as garbage. Such giving does not attract God's blessing. Moreover, being generous to only those who can afford your favor is a common human tactic; even unbelievers exercise the habit. Jesus said,

Unless your righteousness surpasses the righteousness that is common to the world, you will not enter the kingdom of heaven.[333]

Give to the one who asks you, and do not turn away from the one who wants to borrow from you.[334]

If you love those who love you, what reward will you get? Are not even the tax collectors doing that? And if you greet only your brothers, what are you doing more than the others? Do not even pagans do that? Be perfect, therefore, as your heavenly Father is perfect.[335]

When you pray, "Forgive us our sins for we also forgive everyone who sins against us; and lead us not into temptation, but deliver us from the evil one;" you must ask God to favor the entire world. Divine forgiveness involves more than pardon. Ordinary pardon averts punishment but not guilt. When God forgives, He also averts guilt.

The seriousness of guilty sinners facing eternal death should never be underestimated. A perished person has guilt, which he or she cannot amend. Jesus taught us to ask God's forgiveness so that His Spirit may always lead us to bypass temptations. Humanity's sin hinders the effect of God's power at work. By asking God's forgiveness, we advance our request for personal happiness to include advancement of God's kingdom. Forgiveness is an important cornerstone of peace; it has the nature of give and take.

The Lord's Prayer is a commitment—it obligates you to forgive those who have offended you, which will help you enjoy life in God's presence. Peter asked Jesus Christ how many times he must forgive anyone who offended him. Jesus replied,

333   Matt. 5:20
334   Matt. 5:42
335   Matt. 5:46–48

At least seventy-seven times per day.[336]

By saying seventy-seven times per day, Jesus pointed to universal reconciliation. Bearing no grudge against anybody is a precondition to true worship. Neither Peter, nor anyone else, should keep track of how many times we forgive. We should always forgive those who are truly repentant, despite the number of times they ask to be forgiven.

With regard to public worship, Jesus said,

If you are offering your gift at the altar and there remembered that your brother has something against you, first go and be reconciled to your brother, then come and offer your gift.[337]

The central emphasis of Jesus' ministry was forgiveness; accordingly, none of the New Testament writers dwelled on guilt. The courage to perform the works of the Lord's Prayer is equally important to all believers. The significance is not because we are serious sinners but because we all must work seriously to improve our relation with God.

---

336   Matt. 18:21–22
337   Matt. 5:23–24

Chapter 5

⚜

Teaching and Worship

God shows the world that we have a great sense of historical obligation in the inspiration that gave way to the Bible. We are obligated to understand our history and appreciate who we are. God shows us that this is the case by inspiring the authors of the Bible to record it. The Bible is the testimony of real people, and it reveals the pattern of God's relationship with His people. The historical process of salvation is emotionally satisfying, except to the children of the evil one—those who Satan won to himself by their disapproval of God.

The essence of historical theological study is to learn what the truth implies and follow its pattern. The Bible contains divine wisdom, which the apostle Paul described as the secret wisdom of God destined for believers' glory even before time began. Biblical history reveals the depth of God's purpose; and God's purpose is not just historical but true for all ages.[338] His divine wisdom renders the wisdom of this world inadequate in that God is not of any age.

---

338   1 Cor. 2:7

God's secret wisdom was once hidden, but now it is made known to believers. His secret remains hidden to unbelievers of God because of their unbelief:

> *None of the rulers of this world understood it, for if they had, they would not have crucified the Lord of glory.*[339]

Yet, still, they crucify Him in many different ways.

The act of Nehemiah and his associate priest, Ezra, demonstrates the uses of historical theology for spiritual growth and in nation building. After seventy years in exile, the Israelites were allowed to return to their homeland. By returning to the land of Israel from Babylon, the Jews renewed their faith in God's promise to restore them as a people. Ezra and Nehemiah's effective leadership in organizing the return served to rebuild the national and spiritual lives of the people. These men made personal commitments to live for God; they helped the people return to the influence of God's word. Ezra restored the path to spiritual revival by organizing proper teachings of the law soon after the people returned.[340] Ezra and his men read and explained the law to the remnant of the house of Israel:

> *So on the first day of the seventh month Ezra the priest brought the law before the assembly, which was made up of men and women and all who were able to understand. Then he read it aloud from daybreak till noon as he faced the square before the Water Gate, in presence of the men, women, and others who could understand. And all the people listened attentively to the Book of the Law.*[341]

---

339   1 Cor. 2:8
340   Jer. 39; the exilic period lasted for about seventy years.
341   Neh. 8:2–3

Ezra sensed the need to rebuild the shattered spiritual life of the people; and the insight was particularly helpful to those who were born in the exile. Moral chaos existed among the people when Israel had no king and judge to guide them:

Everyone did what was right in his own eyes.[342]

Ezra learned through events of the past how self-guided right and wrong could result moral chaos. He took upon himself the responsibility of leading the people back to the truth.

Nehemiah, who twice served as governor of Judea, was a cupbearer at the palace of Artaxerxes, king of Persia, when the order for him to return from exile was signed. Nehemiah was an exemplary leader and nationalist; while living comfortably in exile, his heart was in Jerusalem. Nehemiah expressed the practical, everyday side of our faith in God. With fasting and prayer, he orchestrated the rebuilding of Jerusalem's wall soon after Israel returned.[343] While Ezra led the revival, Nehemiah used his office as governor and challenged the people to show their faith by their works. The moral contributions by Nehemiah and Ezra show how essential self-sacrifice is to worship, especially in leadership. Both men responded to the problems of the time with prayer and swift action; they had the spiritual readiness that heeds God's call.

Our society is on a difficult bridge because we live by self-guided truth. Individuals and societies have made themselves the final authority in decision making without referencing God. We satisfy our desires at all cost, just as we bear the consequences. Many people gather from the spoils of earthly treasure and ignore the treasures of heaven. The contemporary churchman is in desperate need of

---

342   Judges 21:25
343   Neh. 1–2

moral leadership and spiritual revival. Considering our situation, Christians in pain must not fight to die but live by the hand of God. Earthly death must surely come to pass, but life in Jesus Christ is the miracle that lasts forever.

The grand need of today's pulpit is simply revelatory preaching and nothing less. It is unfaithful to formulate different meanings for biblical messages. You formulate different meanings of biblical message when you change the intended message so as to make it more acceptable and friendly to the listeners.

So far, the acts of Ezra and Nehemiah are kept in the book so that we may imitate their good works. Accordingly, the public reading and explanation of the law brought about a great wave of repentance and revival among the people, as it was the finding of the book of the law that also brought about King Josiah's reform.[344]

The Sense of Good Teaching

Do not consider every truth to be useful, even though all truth will always be true. Some philosophy gives more attention to truth as a property of statement than to the biblical meaning of truth as a personal attribute. The philosophers' viewpoints provide many proposals wherein truths may exist; yet few connect to absolute moral truth. By adding truth to every theory, the real truth is hardly known.

A doctorate of philosophy does not imply that the bearer is all-knowing; rather, it is a testimony that a person may have reached the maximum of a basic understanding familiar to humanity. Philosophical speculation should be limited to things of this earth; we must humble ourselves to divine revelation to benefit from the truth.

---

344   2 Kings 22:11; when King Josiah heard the content of the law he tore his clothes in despair and immediately ordered reform. Through the reform he changed the course of the nation.

Truth refers to God's character—it embodies His dealings with people, the transforming power of Jesus Christ, and the way in which God's people are to deal with everyone. Truth is not identical to human knowledge, and it is not limited. Every teaching has some knowledge to provide, but not all knowledge is worthwhile. Unlike temporal truths of human philosophy, divine truth is the unchanging Spirit source of life—a spring of living water to those who believe in redemption. Divine truth is a commitment to love, for the truth can lead to salvation. Those who set aside the truth have only "unfiltered cistern" to live from.

In every sort of evil that deceives those who are perishing, they perish because they refused to love the truth and so be saved.[345]

Truth has no common quality; only the Spirit can convince one of true meaning. On the account of reviving the remnant of the house of Israel, we read,

Ezra read distinctly from the book, in the law of God, and they gave the sense and helped the people to understand the reading.[346]

We cannot overrate the usefulness of biblical hermeneutics in using the right doctrine to prompt spiritual growth. Ezra and his men joined biblical hermeneutics to good teaching skills, and they made the intent of the law clear.

Refreshing your memory with God's word is a great source of awakening; it is an opportunity to master the truth against the gluts of earthly wisdom. Do not let the truth of His law depart from you;

345   2 Thess. 2:10
346   Neh. 8:8

meditate on it day and night and be careful to do the things that God's word demands.[347]

With regard to the Gospel, true ignorance is forgivable. Jesus said that the end will not come unless everyone truly understands the meaning of God's love and the danger of adopting sin to this temporal life.[348] We must advance the Gospel until the message settles in all corners of the earth, as testimony to God's salvation. Implied ignorance does not include intellectuals and deliberate evildoers who understand God's commandments, but object to them. In some ways, the entire concept of God will continue to lack proper sense to some people. But God has great compassion for those who cannot discern their right hand from their left.

In the story of Jonah's visit to Nineveh, Jonah felt anger toward God when God forgave the sins of the people. Then God replied,

But Nineveh has more than a hundred and twenty thousand people who cannot tell their right hand from their left and many cattle as well. Should I not be concerned about that great city?[349]

Desperate souls yearning for freedom set an exclusive rule for proper teaching. Good Bible interpretation is the only access to God's mind; in it is the power to free oneself from the squeeze of death. We must preach nothing except what already is, and we should establish nothing as true except the truth Himself.[350] Through teaching, praying, or preaching, we must present God's word in the form that it is intended.

---

347   Josh. 1:8
348   "And the Gospel of the Kingdom will be preached in the whole world as a testimony to all nations, and then the end will come" (Matt. 24:14).
349   Jonah 4:11
350   Matt. 28:19–20

To understand the Bible, you must do more than merely read it. Reading the Bible is meaningful, but reading alone often fails to bring about its true meaning and the relationship between different parts of the Bible. Jesus Christ commanded His followers to spread the good news—to teach and guide the world to understand the meaning in ways that help all people remember God's warning and obey His commandments.

No wise person will deliberately rest his or her salvation on the threshold of self-assurance; rather he or she will turn to the gracious mercy of Christ for salvation. The saving truth sets free those who maintain the proper belief. In a familiar way to recognize ourselves, all believers must openly acknowledge allegiance to Jesus Christ by the seal of baptismal water ministered in the authority of the Godhead. The impact toward achieving delightful worship cannot be overrated if Church leaders can, through baptism, cultivate a culture in which the Spirit's influence carries on the oneness of the truth.

Unfortunately, some ministers baptize believers into the union of the Church instead of the union of Christ. For such ministers, baptism by water performed outside their Church's approval is invalid and unacceptable. This attitude cultivates belief through prejudice. We do not save ourselves; and sectarianism does not promote the oneness of God. The Holy Spirit's influence is the difference between freedom and slavery. But when converts are caught in between carnally motivated dispute, they easily lose their progress toward empowerment from the Holy Spirit.

We are not supposed to compel any one to be rebaptized. As a matter of fact, there is no biblical reason for rebaptism. Baptism by water does not save; it is a sign of belief. Commitment to Jesus Christ saves. Baptism by water is an unavoidable expression of belief made before a group of believers. It does not constitute salvation. Rather, it is an outward declaration of inward grace. Infant baptism is as valid as adult baptism, on the condition that the baptized child must demonstrate personal conviction and confession of and commitment to the Lord Jesus Christ at a later age.

According to Paul,

Women will be saved through childbearing—if they continue in faith, love, and holiness with propriety.[351]

Parents have the obligation to make decisions that could secure the spiritual and physical welfare of their children until their children are old enough to manage their own fate. Baptism by water associates confirmation of faith with daily works of righteousness. Without the latter, the concept is useless.

Jesus said,

Go and make disciples of all nations.[352]

If Jesus meant that His followers should make a symbolic gesture of God's salvation to the world, then the task is too easy for this generation. The message has found space on the Internet and in multimedia networks; thereby, Gospel programs generate worldwide awareness. If awareness is all that one needs to be saved, cable television networks could convert thousands of people on each Gospel program and Christians could soon finish the task.

But what about understanding the true meaning of the message, which means commitment to believing in the psychology of Jesus' death on the Cross, that Jesus' death over two thousand years ago concerns the current generations? What about the true meaning that

---

351   1 Tim. 2:15; God instructed, 'Go, multiply, and fill the earth.' Women who fulfill their God given roles are demonstrating true commitment and obedience to Christ.

352   Matt. 28:19

Jesus' death brings personally to every life—the concept that one person can be with millions of people in different places at the same time?

Without true faith, the grace that we hope for may save no one. True faith is the reason the work is ongoing. Ezra's part was not merely teaching the law to the people; he explained every sense of it and helped the people identify with its merits. Likewise, Christians ought to preach the Gospel and, in their interactions with others, demonstrate every sense of the truth to this dying world. To count the number of believers merely by baptism by water is illusive. We owe the world a good explanation of the truth and the motivation to believe and practice the truth.

Teaching alone does not make a complete worship package, but the process can, in practice, fulfill some of the demand. The platform of biblical teaching is obedience; following the trend wherever it may lead is worship. Truth is an identity; those who bear witness to the truth should also bear the mark.

Preaching and Teaching

To some extent, the Gospel is a victim of its own success. Faulty preaching and teaching methods have led to some setbacks in the Church's efforts to inspire godliness in believers. Preaching and teaching result in spiritual growth proportionate to the merits of their methodology. Their effectiveness in sustaining growth depends on how tactfully the preacher or teacher applies the elements of the message.

Preaching and teaching are not one and the same. The two are closely related, but each has a separate rule of engagement. Some Churches teach when they should preach, and they preach in times that call for teaching. Biblical teaching is explaining the truth in scripture—helping listeners to understand difficult passages so as to apply all of God's word to their daily lives. Preaching is proclaiming the word of God—confronting listeners with the truth of scripture so as to motivate them to believe and act according to their beliefs.

The apparent goal of preaching constitutes, in part, the reason preaching requires more emotional power and greater dynamism than teaching. The power of God's word electrifies the emotion of the preacher, and by the influence of the Spirit, the preached message holds the listeners captive and fills the emptiness of their hearts. Prophet Isaiah foretold the influence as 'leveling of rough grounds and making low the hills and mountains.'[353] The rough grounds, hills, and mountains are the many obstacles we must confront; they are the worldliness, trials, and temptations that besiege us, for which we seek God's touch.

A progressive Church carefully separates preaching from teaching and primarily devotes adequate time to applying both concepts to God's worship. Many Churches neglect Bible lessons; but as noted, preaching serves to encourage listeners to hold onto their trust in God's word. The indispensable condition for true preaching is the faithful proclamation of biblical message. Readers may not properly engage with the preached message, if they have received no background information by way of teaching to support the message's claim. Preaching is not grounded in mere repetition of scripture; it must be an explanation of both scripture and real-life situation, so that the living word is heard at the intersection of text and present reality. Likewise, knowledge gained from Bible lesson may not properly assimilate if no empowerment provides for the application, which preaching does.

Teaching is grounded in historical theological study to reflect the truth and circumstances of the background information. Historical theological study has the tendency to settle God's demand in present-day reality.

Take the example of a bride and bridegroom who stood before the altar to take their marriage vows. The bride was asked whether

---

353   Isa. 40: 4 - 5

she accepted the bridegroom in prosperity, poverty, and sickness to be her lawfully wedded husband until death.

She sharply replied, "Oh, no!" Her sharp look told it all. She looked forcefully at the presiding minister and asked, "Must I swear to the liability of such condition before this public? I should have been warned."

The bride reacted ignorantly but honestly. She did not reject marrying her spouse but felt that the question was awkward in public and so directly. Obviously, she was caught unprepared. "It was embarrassing," she said afterward. "I did not expect that anyone would ask a thing like that." She had not thought through the answer she would give, and therefore, she was unable to say "yes" right away.

More could have been done by way of teaching in preparation for the wedding. The young lady may have been listening to Sunday morning sermon, but her ignorance about biblical marriage was a result of factors other than not just listening well.

How best to share with someone the basic knowledge of true faith may depend on how well he or she is christened and whether he or she accepts the usefulness of the Bible to faith. The first step toward helping someone grow in faith is to assess his or her background—to find out how often and why he or she goes to Church. Perhaps the person may go to Church on a regular basis, but his or her major setback is a lack of enthusiastic Bible study.

Church leadership must restore growth into spiritual maturity by introducing biblical patterns of leadership and accountability. Especially in a religion-free society like that of the United States, people like viewing Christianity more simplistically than is accurate—as simply belief in nonviolence; therefore, they adhere only to its moral byproduct. Having drifted away from Christian theology, a good number of Christians do not bother themselves with rediscovering the true meaning of faith. Consequently, these Christians are comfortable with only the social benefits of Christianity. "Christian" in modern expression is nothing more than a decent, civilized, and presentable person.

It is wrong to believe that Christianity mixed with nonviolent secular concepts is not a contradiction. Take the case of the bride as an example. It could be that the bride and bridegroom had no good Christian background and, therefore, no knowledge of the biblical concept of marriage. Perhaps a good teaching about Christian marriage could enable the couple to understand the core of their marital relationship and, thereby, put their vows in the right perspective. They should have received the teaching, at least as counsel, before they get married in the Church.

Yet again, the spiritual problem of the contemporary man of God is centered on tolerance. Church worship is regarded by many ordinary people as an event equivalent to any social gathering. The idea of Church for entertainment makes the system of our worship porous. Non-Christians sometimes prefer to have marriage ceremonies in Church chapels for merely social reasons. I know of non-Christian couples who took their marriage vows in Church and have not been to any Church worship ever since. The reason they chose the house of worship for their wedlock was the impression that weddings performed in a cathedral are more prestigious than those performed in a courtroom or elsewhere.

We must not allow the open-mindedness of this age to take the place of moral theology; and we must not allow the good principles of faith to drown in the ocean of tolerance. Christians are obliged to act friendly to non-Christians, which means to all people, while maintaining strict position of the truth. The fear of God is traditional to Christians; it is the reason to form no defiling alliance with unbelievers.[354] Holiness implies taking serious the nature of our

---

354   2 Cor. 6:14–16

partnership with Jesus Christ in honoring the Father. We must disfavor certain demands for the sake of the judgment.

On a separate occasion, on the road toward Gaza, the Holy Spirit observed an Ethiopian man returning from a pilgrimage to Jerusalem while he read the book of Isaiah on his chariot. The man understood nothing about the passage until the Holy Spirit directed the apostle Philip to go and help him. Philip saw the Ethiopian on his way and he ran up to the man's chariot. Philip asked the man after he heard him reading,

Do you understand what you are reading? And he answered, "How can I understand when no one guides me?"[355]

The feeling of frustration in the Ethiopian's response indicates two things. First, he was bothered by his lack of insight; this suggests that, second, he had an inner desire to learn the truth. The desire reached the attention of the Holy Spirit, and He sent a study guide who led the man to the saving truth.

The man asked Philip,

Tell me, please, who is the prophet talking about; himself or someone else?[356]

Philip was able to guide the man to the truth. The man believed in Jesus Christ and Philip baptized him immediately.[357]

The outcome of the Ethiopian's study could have been different if Philip had not stayed by and helped the Ethiopian. Maybe the man would have read until he finished the entire book of Isaiah, but to no avail.

---

355   Acts 8:30–31
356   Acts 8:34
357   Acts 8:37–38

I have no doubt about the existence of Bible readers like the Ethiopian. Nevertheless, Christians with no Bible of their own are less mindful of the truth. Every Christian should own at least one version of the Holy Bible, which he or she can read and understand. Knowing the Bible begins with study. If the Ethiopian wasn't studying the Bible with determination to learn the truth, the Holy Spirit would not have given him the attention. With devotional study, the scripture becomes spiritual food from which to gain spiritual life. The Bible is eternal and infinite; new aspects of familiar verses will continue to unfold as long as you keep on studying them. More than any intellectual technique, your mind-set will set you on a path of revival when engaging in devotional study. It is more helpful to study the Bible methodically than at random.

Do not hesitate to ask for help if you read and do not understand. There is no shame in asking for help, especially spiritual help. Do not wait for help like the Ethiopian; it may not come quickly enough. Advance your salvation by reaching out to other believers or join any Christian Bible study group around you.

In addition, the Church has a unique responsibility to fish for people like the Ethiopian and help them gain the truth. Jesus Christ had this in mind when He made His followers fishers of men.[358] The task does not imply that you should persuade people to join your brand of Church. Rather, you should help them to unfold the truth in a way that enables the truth to set them free.

Now is our time; we ought to establish our witness to God's work in every corner of the world. Sadly and regrettably, some Christians allow the yoke of Church denomination to prevent them from enjoying Bible study with other Christians. The yoke prevents some gifted Bible teachers from teaching the Bible as lively as they

---

358   Matt. 4:19

ought to. The compound effect of prejudice toward evangelism results in many starving souls being denied the full experience of the Holy Spirit. The victims feel the desperation, the yearning of their souls. And yet they block themselves because of their allegiance to dogma and to the lords of dogma. Jesus referred to such human failure when he said,

The spirit is willing but the flesh is weak.[359]

To conclude the chapter, I will draw slightly from my life experience in order to talk about how proper teaching combined with a good method of Bible study can lead to delightful worship.

My God is Your God

From the time of my mid-childhood to my early adulthood, I pondered over and struggled with a Bible study assignment that my Sunday school teacher gave to the class. The assignment bothered me and, subsequently, changed my perception of God over time. I did not anticipate the outcome that a normal take-home assignment from Sunday school could remarkably captivate my life. However, these were the years of my turning point.

My parents worshipped in an Episcopal Church, called Anglican Church in my part of the world. The Church, located in a remote African village, conducted Bible study on Sunday afternoon for children of various age groups. The Sunday school usually closed at 4.00 p.m. to give way for evening worship before sunset.

On the afternoon that would change my spiritual outlook, the class teacher took the topic of our discussion from Isaiah 46:10, which reads,

---

359   Matt. 26:41

I predicted the end from the beginning, from ancient times what is yet to come. I say, "My word shall stand, and I will do all that I please."[360]

The teacher introduced the verse by saying, "God is unique and all-knowing; He alone controls the future. His consistent purpose carries His plan even to the point where human experience indicates the opposite."

As the study progressed, the teacher cited references from parts of the Bible to make Isaiah's viewpoint clear. He told the class the story of Joseph from the book of Genesis, chapter 37, and explained the connection to God's plan. The theme of the study was "the purposeful God."

"Nothing exists for nothing's sake," the teacher repeatedly told us. "Our God is a purposeful God, and everything that God created has a purpose."

I listened attentively to him and also to the older boys who added their voices to the discussion. The lesson seemed to reach a climax when the teacher linked the discussion to members of the class. I remember him saying, "God's purpose includes everyone. Everyone is made in the image of God, and He knows us by name."

I loved storytelling when I was a boy, and my father was a good storyteller. During early evening when my father would rest from his day's work, I usually stayed next to him and lay my head gently on his chest while we waited for dinner. My father would me tell me stories about the animal kingdom that existed somewhere in the jungle. My father's art of storytelling gave me my first sense of and youthful opinion about the Bible—a fine book by another fine storyteller. Having been told by my father that the Bible is the word of God, my infant brain could carry me no further than to reach the

---

360   Isa. 46:10

assumption that God must be a good storyteller. My only thought about God was when I would meet with Him. I learned that He live in heaven and sees everything on this Earth.

Little by little, I developed a heart for God, especially because my father told me that everyone will one day appear in heaven to meet with God's presence. I paid attention in Sunday school so that I could hear more about God's stories as told by those who understand His personality. I did not imagine, at least as a child, that God's story and its purpose is something personal.

At the end of the Sunday school class, we went home with an assignment. The teacher asked every one of us to search for the purpose that we were made and decide what steps to take so as to fulfill the purpose. My first flash of thought was to ask my parents. After that, my young mind focused on the various things I might be in future. Take-home studies were part of the Sunday school program and usually not too difficult to solve, but this particular assignment was stuck in my mind. The more I tried to solve the assignment, the more I realized that the future was not clearly marked. The future, then, was practically unforeseeable and had no convincing answer for my assignment. I wanted something more concrete to connect to God, but I found nothing.

My passion for God increased as a result. I needed to hear more about God and possibly from God Himself; I needed to hear what His purpose and this life meant.

I felt surprisingly disappointed when my parents told me that they had no answer to what the future might be but that God knew. In an effort to help me understand my mother once said, "We bore you as our son, but your existence is God's making, not ours. You are a gift to us, and your destiny is in God's hand."

According to my father, "Our part is to parent your upbringing in the best possible way and in things of the Lord. You must make up the rest of your life using God's help."

As years passed, I realized that I could not convince myself of any practical answer to that assignment. I wanted to find the solution to the assignment before I graduated, at least to impress my Sunday school teacher. It seemed to me, to a point, that the effort was meaningless if all that I wanted is to impress my Sunday school teacher. So I decided to use the occasion to learn more about myself while I contemplated my father's verdict that I must make up the rest of my life by myself.

Everything about this life pointed to God, but I could not find Him to solve the puzzle in my head. Within the school years, my mind ran over many options, but none sounded convincing to my spirit. My desire for an answer grew to slight anxiety when my parents could not satisfactorily assist me. They encouraged me to study hard in school and pray always that God may reveal Himself to me. I escaped myself later on by ignoring the assignment. Luckily, the teacher never asked what our resolves were.

Because of my curiosity, the assignment never left me. I could feel the burden lingering inside me, especially when I thought about my future. The assignment was like a closed fire inside; I could feel the anxiety on crossroads to major life decisions. Sometimes, I felt like the Sunday school class had never ended. I remembered what was said in the class, and I imagined possible implications of the discussion. *Does God know where I am now and what I am doing?* I asked myself. *Can it be true that God from the ancient time of Adam and Eve knows who I am, when I was born, and the land where I was born?* I wondered if God chose my parents for me or if it had just happened that I was born to them. *If there is a purpose to my existence, what is it?* I wondered.

My desire to find honest answers to these questions did two things in my life. I developed an appetite to discover the true meaning of humanity, and I learn more from the Bible about God, especially to discover the purpose for which He created all things.

The passion increased my desire to listen whenever God was the topic of discussion.

But the more I listened and studied the Bible, the more I discovered many unanswered questions; I especially wondered why God inspired the Bible writers to tell the world the things in the Bible and why everybody needed to hold true to His word.

Other relative viewpoints about God gradually become a matter of my personal interest; and some of the opinions I sought out and listened to were quite helpful. Subsequently, I began to add my voice to the discussions, sharing with people the little I knew about God. It was not easy for me at school, especially with some high school mates who knocked me out of my defense of God's purpose. Like Nehemiah,

> *I told them of the hand of my God and His goodness to me and also my father's words, which he spoke to me.*[361]

But my classmates laughed my proclamations off. Their parodist attitude challenged me to often return to the Bible for more answers.

It had been my longing since I left that Sunday school to know more about God and share my experiences with other people. On the other hand, I wanted to retain my father's art of storytelling as our family heritage.

Something serious happened to my passion when I realized that God's purpose concerning my life was the exact purpose that concerns everyone. It was the greatest miracle of my life to realize that I did not choose God. He chose me by creating me in His likeness. God's desire to advance His work of righteousness through my lifetime was the answer to my assignment. I sought to know this truth for years and nearly mistook His goal as an inherited fairy tale.

---

361   Neh. 2:18

The answer came to me not exactly like my father told me it would. I found God here on Earth, even though I still look forward to meeting Him in person in heaven. The kingdom of heaven is not far from anyone who listens to the voice of the Holy Spirit.

My passion for more knowledge of God guided me to my career choice, and, subsequently, I took up theological studies in college. It was during my days in seminary that I fully realized that nothing could give me joy like serving and glorifying God in everything that I do. The ability to glorify God and the willingness to show obedience to His instructions is worship. The attitude neither brags nor despises; serving God is the only reason for us to exist. We can serve God and glorify Him in all our activities.

My Sunday school teacher helped me to correct the way I perceived God; and now I uphold the reality of what I discovered. The assignment provoked the spirit that discovers God in me; and I feel His nearness through every struggle. Everyone may not experience God the same way that I do, and everyone may not gain the opportunity to serve God in his or her career that way like I do.

What is true for everyone is that no one can truly afford to set God aside. Denying His hand in your life does not make sense. He predicted the end from the beginning, and His word stands to the end of all things. You hardly live when you do not seek to know your creator; people can exist without living at all.

The assignment led me to much processing and across many lifetime bridges, but it finally gave me the meaning that I wanted— the understanding of God's purpose.

Painful experience is usually a doorway to new opportunities. In many ways, Christianity is not a passive religion that advocates waiting for God to act. Hard work, sacrifice, and doing what we know is right and best for any situation are parts of the Christian discipline. We model our values; and parents in particular demonstrate to their children what they consider valuable. Children often follow the lifestyle of their parents, repeating their successes and mistakes as they grow.

A healthy family is the best possible training environment for children. Children take their clues by watching how their parents honor God and each other. Good family upbringing is a gift; one generation can pass it to the next.

On the other hand, lack of natural care provides harmful examples, which eventually turn against society:

If anyone does not provide for his relatives, and especially for his immediate family, he has denied the faith, and is worse than an unbeliever.[362]

Teaching rooted in reality is more likely to have a positive impact on peoples' lives than empty fable. Our generation had developed itching ears and turned away the living truth. Many people do not endure sound doctrine, living instead according to their desires. They have mind-sets that seek out myth and empty philosophy:

They gather around them a great number of teachers to say what their itching ears want to hear.[363]

They want truth that makes sense to what they feel, what works for them, and what seems compelling, to which they claim absolute right. They gather viewpoints that suit their selfish desires and profess objectivity that only defends the viewpoints.

Against these constructs, Jesus wants us to imitate His teaching and spiritual standing. Jesus' teachings have great impact on many listeners, especially where His wisdom explains the riddles of real-life

---

362   1 Tim. 5:8
363   2 Tim. 4:3

situations. His teaching touched the people who heard Him, and they said among themselves:

> *There was never a time when we heard a man teach like this.*[364]
> *The people were amazed at His teaching because He taught them as one who had authority, not as the teachers of the law.*[365]
> *As Jesus was saying these things, a woman in the crowd called out, "Blessed is the mother who gave you birth and nursed you."*[366]

On another occasion, Jesus was preaching and the Pharisees sent officers of the Roman guard to arrest Him. The guards went, listened to Jesus, and came out with this complaint:

> *No one has ever spoken like Him before.*[367]

Not without Affordable Risk

If you are able to communicate your faith clearly to another person, you have demonstrated teaching at its best. In measuring your ability to teach, do not consider how many discussions you have had, but ask how much truth you passed on to even one person whom God has brought your way. Believers are open to many ways to serve God; in practice each person must not choose them all. Teaching requires trust and building trust starts with affordable risk. A teacher who initiates a good relationship with those in the process of learning is ideal. He or she is a teachable teacher, who engages in constant learning in order to do better teaching work. A good teacher is

---

364   "Not until halfway through the Feast did Jesus go up to the temple courts and begin to teach. The Jews were amazed and asked, 'How did this man get such learning without having studied?'" (John 7:14–15).

365   Mark 1:22

366   Luke 11:27

367   John 7:46

humble and reconciling and sees the reality of teaching from the difficulty in learning. He builds relationships of trust through the path of wisdom. She does not tolerate laziness but tenderly assists all learning processes. The teacher is a good listener who stimulates learning by showing only the good side of knowledge.

The situation in the Church of Ephesus shows Bible readers how to encourage these qualities in themselves, using Paul and Timothy's relationship as an example. The apostle Paul appointed Timothy to remain in Ephesus and help correct the problem of false teaching in the Church. Ephesus was a wealthy city, and the Ephesians' Church probably had many wealthy members who assumed that they could do and teach whatever they felt.

In his letter to Timothy, Paul wrote,

As I urged you when I went into Macedonia, stay there in Ephesus so that you may charge certain men not to teach false doctrines any longer, nor devote themselves to fables and endless genealogies. These promote disputes rather than God's work, which is by faith. Now the purpose of this command is love which comes from a pure heart, and a good conscience, and a sincere faith.[368]

Paul initiated the teaching process by identifying the problem of the Church. He anticipated the difficulty in Timothy's task and involved Timothy in the teaching and learning process. Timothy was then inexperience and young. Paul charged him with building up teaching and learning relationships with the Church. Part of the strategy was to show the members that having riches carries greater responsibility.

In order for Timothy to learn how to accomplish the task, he had to pay attention to Paul and understand his guidelines. Paul advised

---

368   1 Tim. 1: 3–5

Timothy to be humble. Paul's guideline to Timothy included how to identify what was central to teaching the Bible:

- Reject teachings based on work[369]
- Reject human knowledge that denies faith
- Denounce immoral acts that exist in the Church[370]
- Depend on the use of your spiritual gift
- Be effective in loving and strong in grace[371]
- Preach the truth of sound doctrine in order to convince and rebuke bad attitudes[372]
- Do not be ashamed of the Gospel[373]
- To succeed, you must lead by example[374]

All believers, even if they never plan to be Church leader, should follow these guidelines. To put the guidelines in perspective, Paul wrote in his second letter to Timothy:

All of scripture is God-breathed and useful for teaching, rebuking, correcting, and training in righteousness, so that the man of God may be thoroughly equipped for every good work.[375]

Paul seems to imply two things with the statement. First, he affirms God's active involvement in writing the scripture—an involvement so powerful and pervasive that what is written is infallible and authoritative. Second, he suggests that the personal

---

369   1 Tim. 4:3–5
370   1 Tim. 6:20–21
371   2 Tim. 2:1
372   2 Tim. 4:2
373   2 Tim. 1:8
374   2 Tim. 1:13–14
375   2 Tim. 3:16–17

life of a minister ought to be pure like the doctrine. He did not suggest that ministers must be faultless but that they should be truly dedicated to the good work. A minister's life and the teaching are two elements that are meant for each other. Faithful ministers should be supported; too often ministers are targets of criticism because some congregation has unrealistic expectations.

Nevertheless, the biblical model of leadership is that of servant leader. A servant leader does not boss, dominate, or dictate to God's people. Instead a servant leader asks God's people to do that which God's word has established by exemplifying God's word in his own life. This should be evident in the way he deals with sin and manifest in his spirit of repentance.

Perfectionism is not a requirement in serving the Lord. We should avoid the Pharisees' approach to leadership that calls for not instructing people to do things that we will not do. Servants of the Lord should keep themselves within the life changing process, which the Holy Spirit initiated when they were called. Otherwise, the flock may occasionally appear holier than the shepherd.

Like Saul before he became the apostle Paul, a minister may be totally sinful and inexperienced when the Lord calls him, but his openness to the Holy Spirit's influence revives him to go after God's heart. Serving the Lord faithfully is not being the person you are but being the person you become in the Lord. All people who are open to the Holy Spirit's work of revival have the potential to serve God in many special ways. If God decides to make someone His special instrument, the dust of sin, no matter how thick, cannot withhold the call.

Paul told Timothy that servants of the Lord must not depend on earthly wisdom to discern spiritual things. Otherwise, they risk following fuzzy doctrine. Listen to your inner self and submit to God's influence, which you can access both through the Holy Spirit and conscience. Paul describes the effect as being alive in the Spirit:

So I say, live by the Spirit and you will not gratify the desires of the sinful nature. For the sinful nature desires what is contrary to the Spirit and the Spirit what is contrary to the sinful nature. They are in conflict with each other, so that you do not do what you want. But if you are led by the Spirit, you are not under law.[376]

Servants of God must be careful not to confuse gut feeling with the Holy Spirit's lead. Discernment between feeling and His prompting is an important task of leadership. The Holy Spirit can depart from a minister as a result of the minister's arrogance. By diminishing the calling, the office concludes by losing the intense godliness. Prophet Samuel said to King Saul,

Rebellion is like the sin of divination, and arrogance like the sin of idolatry. Because you have rejected the word of the Lord, He has rejected you as king.[377]

Holiness does not reject what God approves; holiness justifies those who rightly use what God calls good to benefit missionary work. The source of holiness is a personal and practical relationship with God, not a system of work. The source relates to the new covenant in referring to holiness as both personal and collective experience. The guideline to Timothy is, accordingly, a process to develop him and the people at the same time. The Church of Ephesus and its leadership would attain holiness while they maintain the same quality in their private lives.

Paul called the result

---

376   Gal. 5:16–18
377   1 Sam. 15: 23

Bearing fruit in every good work. Growing in the knowledge of God, being strengthened with all power according to His glorious might, so that you may have great endurance and patience, and joyfully giving thanks to the Father who qualified you to share in the inheritance of the saints in the kingdom of light.[378]

Paul knew that desiring knowledge could lead one to changing his or her life.[379] Accordingly, Timothy did all things by Paul's instruction.

The Gospel is not simply about forgiveness. Rather, it is about the totality of returning back to the original people that God created us to be. Humanity is dysfunctional in all attributes of God as a result of sin. Yet admitting that we are not perfect does not cancel out our efforts toward achieving saintly life. Satan works to keep everyone committing sin, in order to prevent spiritual revival. Satan knows that, through devotion to biblical commandments, revival could produce in us the power to reclaim our authority. In other words, sin is a major barrier to biblical fellowship. We can subdue Satan and force growth when we hold, at every turning point, to the biblical direction given by God. In using both your spiritual and mental weapon against the evils around you, be not bothered by their everyday manifestation; God has proposed an end time to all Satan's work.

For all practical purposes, you should experience the Bible as God is speaking to you. The word of God is the shield of your faith; no one can have workable faith without having the word. You are the prophet of your life if your knowledge of the word protects you against the sword of the evil one. If you

---

378   Col. 1:10–14
379   1 Tim. 4:16

can understand God's word spoken in the Bible, how people may perceive and treat you will not influence your action and judgment. If you have the word in you, your emotional thought will be protected with the word. Some Bible statements are directed to particular individuals and groups of people, but all of scripture is relevant to all persons. So that they could find fulfillment in the achievement of a just and happy life, God gave the children of Israel law:

Six days you shall labor, but on the seventh day you shall not labor.[380]

The law is a direct command to the children of Israel, and it is relevant in authority to all of us.

It is the duty of the Holy Spirit to activate God's truth in every mind and connect the relevance of that truth to life's situations. However, our responsibility is to maintain the light of God's truth within us and apply the truth from the context in which it is written. Devotional Bible study can, with prayer, produce sanctity and solution to problems. The good outcome of feeding the soul with spiritual food is the working of God's mercy. Miracles happen by both faith and the authority of His word.

Delightful worship involves using the Bible to its fullest potential, which could trigger in a person the eagerness to seek God's mind. A right and wrong method to Bible study depends on the person or persons involved in the study. Meditative approach is ideal for an independent mind; the method enables the reader to spiritualize the reading. By faith, one can make spiritual connections that address his or her problem using related study passage. It is essential in times

---

380   "But the Sabbath day is the day of the Lord your God, in it you shall do no work" (Ex. 20:8–10).

of need to relate the study of passages to life's situations; solution to problems may depend on it.[381]

However, the approach does not apply as strictly to group study because interpersonal experience applies within a group. Several relative suggestions are necessary in a mixed group to reach everyone's interest. Explaining certain passages to mixed groups may also require various examples. A community group in a Church of Central Africa may require a more familiar example in order to understand Bible verses like Isaiah 1:18 and Psalm 68:14, which refer to snow. The necessity for using a different example will not apply in parts of the world where snowfall is common.

The primary aim of teach-study method is spiritual gain. A technical approach can help Bible readers handle the truth more accurately, but it may not necessarily lead to spiritual growth. Exercising teach-study is a "one step at a time" method, which guides participants to understand and remember God's command. The Bible is primarily a spiritual book to be better understood by spiritual minds. Teach-study method is literal, but the effectiveness in solving spiritual need, especially among local Church communities, is outstanding.

Mixed and local study group largely represent a setting that does not require an immense academic knowledge of the Bible to grow in things of God. Teaching can enhance relationships by encouraging spirituality.

Negative results of scholarly approach to Bible study make me discourage taking theological studies courses in certain schools.

---

381   God is all-powerful and all-knowing. Yet He has chosen to let us help Him change the world through prayers. Bible study that is done through meditation is more beneficial to personal growth; the method feeds the spirit with nourishment and involves the heart more than any intellectual technique. How this works is misery to us because of limited knowledge, but the experience is real.

It is a mistake to study the Bible as dry history and miss the deep personal feelings. Even in a good seminary setting, theorizing the truth can render both teachers and students spiritually empty. Scholarly approach to Bible study is the cause of many seminarians losing their passion for God. Theories are endless illusions made of studies that do not take into account the true message and intent of the Bible writers. I would rather live by Church tradition than live with biased, theoretical viewpoints against the Bible.

Nevertheless, some study groups still require the academic approach to some degree, as it can be a necessary part of eliminating doubt. This does not necessarily mean we should put the truth on trial. Rather, we should seek clarification. Christians should not read the Bible with the academic curiosity of a student of antiquities; and they should not survey historical theological studies with the detachment of a spectator.

Cultural and social mentalities play major roles in determining the methods by which to study the Bible. The truth is an absolute; the outcome of any good Bible study method will not affect the truth; rather, it will result in participants having good knowledge from all grounds. Some societies of believers are primarily interested in the moral and spiritual message of any given passage. To these people, fact is of little importance. If they cannot connect to the moral and spiritual value of a passage, then they assume the passage is meaningless. In other societies, demand for fact and proof of evidence are inevitable. These people consider fact first before evaluating whatever moral and spiritual sense a passage may contain. If the highlights that prove a passage authentic are lost in the study, they may take the passage as unrealistic. In other words, in some societies of believers, all that the truth represents is ethics, whereas in other societies, it is the realness and the applicability of scripture that entice the people. In order to retain everybody's interest in studying the Bible, leaders must connect to the balance.

The difficulty in teaching the Bible in some societies can be as complicated as unlocking certain myths that rule over their world. From my cultural background and through discussions with many contacts around the world, I've realized that the truth can be less useful if it shows no moral value. I've noticed also that the truth can be used in testimony to polish hypocrisy. It is not a serious problem that methods to Bible study may vary; by all accounts, no good method faults the truth. Every Bible study requires a plan.

Study problems are not a result of there not being things we can learn from the Bible but of things we know. Being overly familiar aids no further careful study of many Bible passages; therefore we cannot easily make new discoveries. Observe carefully any passage of your study. Take into account the structure and the character of the text while you read the passage. This will lead the brain to new understanding at each studying point. By observing the character of a text, you will visualize certain facts, which are important to uncovering the intended meaning of the passage. The fact available in a passage helps to reveal its meaning. Observation takes into account all of the terms involved in a passage, from the smallest letter to its relationship with the entire structure of the book. One needs to carefully observe in order to discover the mind of the writer—why the writer wrote the way he did and what purpose the Holy Spirit intended to accomplish through the writing. The writer's grammatical structure and the historical background of the writing are guides to unlocking the work and whatever messages the Holy Spirit is giving.

Remember, the entire Bible is inspired by the Holy Spirit. To get good results from Bible study, you must study with the intention of discovering God's mind, which is more rewarding than any other property of the book. New understanding of biblical wisdom relates to the progress of any study. You need to know and understand the basic message and background information of many parts of the Bible in order to effectively communicate a part of the Bible. The

Bible books are interconnected; their message relates the same goal and gives confidence to witness.

Consider the following observation made from the book of Jonah, chapter 1, and study through the entire book to uncover the intended message. You may discover God's mind telling all generations the story and perhaps grasp more points for application.

Here are a few study guidelines:

1. "Nineveh was a great city." God mentioned this twice in the book.
2. God commanded that Jonah should go and preach to the people.
3. God resolved that Nineveh should know His mind and show His interest in the people.
4. Jonah intended to flee from God, at least to get away from God's known territory to a gentile city called Tar-shish. Jonah did not want to go to Nineveh so he boarded a ship to get away from God. What does the behavior of Jonah, a prophet of God, say to you about his understanding of God?
5. The people on board believed in gods; they were not atheists. Can you perceive the minds of people on board through the passage?
6. By Jonah's disobedience, the people on board were made to experience the power of the Almighty God. Is it true?
7. Jonah explained to the people:

   I am a Hebrew and I worship the Lord, the God of heaven, who made the sea and the land.[382]

   In what way did Jonah's confession of faith affect the people's attitude?

---

382   Jonah 1: 9

8. The people on board were forced by the situation to make promises to the Almighty God. Was their action contradictory to their beliefs?

9. It is possible that some people on the ship converted as a result of the experience. How plausible is the concept?

10. Jonah recognized himself as the cause of the tempest. Did acknowledging the problem help his disobedience in any way?

11. Jonah offered himself to be thrown off the ship. Was his offer more prophetic than an ordinary view of his stubbornness?

12. The people on board did not immediately welcome Jonah's offer as a solution to the problem; they know it would be mean to send Jonah to his death. On whose fear were they reluctant to throw Jonah to the sea and why?

13. The people sought God's exoneration; they recognized Jonah both as a man of God and as one in conflict with his God. Do you notice similar situations in the Church?

14. The difference about Jonah's God and the gods the people on board were accustomed to knowing is made clear to all on board, and they greatly feared Him. Analyze this point using personal experience of God's revelation and salvation.

15. For the ship to be in close contact with the big fish that swallowed Jonah, it could have been sailing on high seas. Even at the point of death, Jonah did not show any fear. The people on board were terrified. Why wasn't Jonah also afraid?

16. Nineveh received a warning that they should patch up their attitudes or face the consequences. Notably, the Bible predicts all that we need to know about our position on Earth and the end-time. Is there anything in the story to suggest that the people of Nineveh were wiser than those of our generation?

17. The book of Jonah shows God as both a punishing and delivering God. Chapter 2 indicates that Jonah probably knew he would not die if he were thrown to the sea. But why did the situation occur if Jonah knew that God would save his life?[383]

A comprehensive step to the exercise is to answer the question, why Nineveh? Who were the people to Israel? Maybe the answer will explain why God was interested in Nineveh—either to save or destroy it. The lifestyles of the people of Nineveh and their attitude toward Israel may help you realize why Jonah refused to preach to the people and why the people took upon them Jonah's message. Our share in the story constitutes, yet again, God's mind reminding us about a people like Nineveh.

---

383   "Then I said, 'I have been cast out of your sight; yet I will look again toward your holy temple'" (Jonah 2:4).

Chapter 6

The Desert Church

The Gospel is more dynamic when we understand the history and the culture involved in the events it describes. Reading the New Testament writing without the knowledge of the Old Testament prevents the reader from important background information, which unlocks the message. As one theologian said, reading the New Testament without knowledge of the Old Testament is like coming into a play in the middle and not fully grasping what is going on.

With regard to the book of the prophets, we must study and understand the prophecies so as to know what the situations were at the time, what the people thought, the relationships between countries, and the attitude in which the people responded to God and each of the prophecies. Doubts about divine mind-set on covenants and law, tithe and priesthood, sin, and God's wrath are rectifiable by examining their roots in the Old Testament. When the apostle Paul spoke of Jesus Christ as the sacrifice of atonement, he was not inventing a new concept. The theology was built on a firm foundation of God's revelation through the law and the prophets. The Old Testament provides the knowledge of God's unfolding plan from the beginning of His work with humanity. The event, which includes the study of the beginning, provides a foundation for what is and what comes later. The content presents subject matters that authenticate the seriousness of sin and the faithfulness of God in fulfilling His promise of redemption. The highlights are lessons of moral principle for all believers, and the outline gives a concise picture of consequence to all human misbehavior.

Study of Old Testament theology reveals God's capacity to love and bless and to judge and punish. It is often pointed out, sadly from the pulpit itself, that the God of the Old Testament is a jealous God—a God of wrath and judgment—whereas the Christian God is the God of forgiveness and love. Without the awareness of divine wrath and judgment, the experience of God's love easily lapses into a kind of sticky sentimentality, as in many modern worship songs. Without the knowledge of God's wrath, the hope of divine forgiveness loses its redemptive significance.

The book of Lamentation, for instance, concerns a national disaster that is recognizable as God's judgment, yet the writer proclaims,

Because of the Lord's great love we are not consumed, for His compassions never fail. God's mercies are new every morning and form the reason to hope and quietly wait for His salvation.[384] *Why should any living man complain when punished for his sins? Let us examine our ways and test them, and let us return to the Lord.*[385]

The God who spoke through Jesus Christ freely offered humanity His forgiveness. Yet the revelation of His love prompted Christians like the apostle Paul to say,

---

384   Lam. 3:22–26
385   Lam. 3:39–40

The wrath of God is being revealed from heaven against all unrighteousness of men, who suppress the truth by their wickedness.[386]

God's anger from the beginning was that people joined Satan to substitute truth with lies.

They exchanged the truth of God for a lie and worship and serve created things rather than the Creator—who is forever praised. Amen."[387]

From both the Old and the New Testaments, the morally perfect God neither tolerates sin nor ignores willful rebellion. God wants to remove sin and restore the sinner, as long as the sinner does not stubbornly distort or reject the truth. God's revelation to Moses is consistent with the prophets and Jesus Christ in revealing God's mercy and justice:

And the Lord passed in front of Moses proclaiming, "The Lord, the Lord, the compassionate and gracious God, slow to anger, abounding in love and faithfulness, maintaining love to thousands, and forgiving wickedness, rebellion, and sin. Yet, He does not leave the guilty unpunished; He punishes the children and their children for the sin of the fathers to the third and fourth generation of those dishonoring Him.[388]

Since the beginning of the New Testament era, the Holy Spirit is more evident in helping believers to better understand the Gospel and respond to its message. His work does not rule out historical

---

386   Rom. 1:18
387   Rom. 1:25
388   Ex. 34:6–7

background material. The Old Testament shows how the ancient, inspired Hebrew writers expressed the narrative about God's saving deeds. The Holy Spirit brings to fulfillment the promised salvation in the newly created community of saints and embraces Jews and Gentiles to jointly accept His missionary task. As Christians, we must embrace the Old Testament as our spiritual history. The promise to and the calling of Israel are also our historical promise and calling. The New Testament era is the second level of the story of God redeeming a people for His name's sake, which when properly applied, helps us to understand the sub-Christian nature of the Old Testament believers. As we read the Old Testament stories of God's saving grace, the understanding helps us to find our place within the history; we can see the way God wants us to mold our behavior and define our identity as believers. The Old Testament narrative connects us with the ability to solve the moral and spiritual problems of our time and fulfills how we proclaim the biblical stories in plain meaning and in terms familiar in our cultures.

God raised the nation of Israel to lead His worship—to be the kingdom of priests among the nations of the world. Old Testament theology demonstrates God's proposed worship as the theme of the redemption plan. The story about the Desert Church tells the outcome of God's persistence in history; it demonstrates how He counters humanity's sin. God had every person in mind when He created the universe:

For He chose us in Him before the creation of the world to be holy and blameless in His sight. In love He predestined us to be adopted as His children through Jesus Christ in accordance with His pleasure and will.[389]

---

389   Eph. 1:4–5

The doctrine of creation tells humanity's glory from the standpoint of God's plan. By contrast, the viewpoint of evolution theory to human origin represents total fallacy and further degrades humanity's intellectual and social integrity. The image of science is robotic; science has no means of determining moral right and wrong. Not so long ago, the glory of scientific discovery told us that the earth was flat. We are not beasts on the planet; all work of creation, with the apparent risks, is the work of God's sovereignty. Every basic life and the physical world are created to a unique function of His worship:

> *The heavens rejoice, the sea and everything in it resounds, the fields and everything in them are jubilant, all the trees of the forest swing with pleasure, the rivers clap their hands, the mountains sing together for joy, and they all sing to the glory of the Lord.*[390]
> *But ask the animals, and they will teach you, or the birds of the air, and they will tell you; or speak to the earth, and it will teach you, or let the fish of the sea inform you. Which of all these does not know that the hand of the Lord has done this? In His hand is the life of every creature and the breath of all mankind.*[391]

Nothing of the universe came out of nowhere, and we can only boast of what is revealed. The breath of life received its profound meaning in the Creator's intent.

Evolution theory is worth no second thought. The Bible has already provided the missing link to perfection, about which the theory is trying hard to speculate. Superior understanding and the consciousness of the Most High God qualify humanity as moral

---

390   Ps. 96:11–12; Ps. 98:7–8
391   Job 12:7–10

creatures. Unfortunately, the kingdom of darkness is desperate. Those who reject God's word are bound to seek inferior explanations to their questions. Evolution theory is an open-ended exercise and exists in neither fact nor realism.

Therefore, see to it that no one takes you captive through hollow and deceptive philosophy, which depends on human tradition and the basic principles of this world, rather than on Christ.[392]

While the Bible is not primarily about science, it is accurate where it deals with science and its anti-God mentality. No book or system of belief except the Bible can give its followers the power to change their lives to true goodness. The positions of scientific culture are very attractive, but we must consider God's perspective if we are to have a proper view of the universe. God rules by the principle of delegated authority. He has full control of everything visible and invisible, and He is forever king:

To God belong wisdom and power; counsel and infinite understanding are His. What He tears down cannot be rebuilt; the man He imprisons cannot be released. If He holds back the waters, there is drought; if He lets them loose, they devastate the land. To Him belong strength and victory.[393]

So deep is God's sovereignty that He is able to transform the wrath of men into praise for Him. His enemies end up serving Him in spite of themselves. When Adam and Eve first sinned, God began His judgment with the Serpent.[394] He used the protoevangel

---

392   Col. 2:8
393   Job 12:13–16
394   Gen.3:14–15; Gal. 4:4; Rev. 20:2

to announce His intention to redeem the world. The rest of the Old Testament reveals the progressive development of a twofold plan. God chose two men of faith through whom He set His program in motion. The first was Abraham, who lived about 2000 BC; the next was King David, whose seed, the anointed One, is the savior of the world.

God's Purpose in Calling Abraham

God called Abraham out of his homeland in Ur of the Chaldeans[395] and established a new covenant of worship with him. God told Abraham to go to the land of Canaan, which would be Abraham's inheritance.[396] The divine agenda was the forthcoming of God's gracious response to the fornications of the generations of Babel, who according to their groups have scattered across the face of the earth.[397]

Abraham took his wife, Sarah, and his nephew, Lot, and they traveled from Ur by way of Haran to the land of Canaan. Faith drove Abraham to believe all of God's promise.

Abraham lived as stranger in the land and did not witness in his lifetime the fulfilling of the promise. The Lord said to him,

You, however, will go to your fathers in peace and be buried at a good old age.[398]

---

395   Gen. 11:31; Ur is located in southern part of modern-day Iraq.
396   "Now the Lord said to Abram, 'Get out of your country, from your family and from your father's house, to the land that I will show you'" (Gen. 12:1–3).
397   "So the Lord scattered them from there over all the earth, and they stopped building the city. That is why it was called Babel—because there the Lord confused the language of the whole world. From there the Lord scattered them over the face of the whole earth" (Gen.11:8–9). (Gen. 10:4; from there, the maritime people spread out into their territories by their clans within their nations, each with its own language.)
398   Gen.15:15

Nevertheless, God ensured that Abraham understood that his descendants were the pioneers of the blessing:

I will make you into a great nation and I will bless you; I will make your name great, and you will be a blessing. I will bless those who bless you, and whoever curses you I will curse; and all peoples on Earth will be blessed through you.[399]

Abraham is an example of faith that did not fail; he walked lengths of a difficult process to stand in a unique position, as the father of a nation and the father of all believers.

Faith fails when passion retreats from supporting the actions of faith. God, for His part, fulfills His promise even when no human action supports His purpose. The proposed worship order, first among Abraham's offspring and then the rest of the world, has the strength of character to lead all nations of the earth to worship God. The unique worship system allows grace to descend and erase the effects of sin.

Humanity is, to a degree, immortal; yet God set eternity in the human soul.[400] God is not concerned about whether the human soul will live forever; rather He is concerned with where the soul will spend eternity. Physical death makes way for transition into the afterlife, yet sin compels a majority of the death to the wrong end. Having fallen to sin, human beings cannot spend eternity in God unless something is done to redeem them of sin. The ultimate value of salvation is not what we are saved from but what we are saved for:

Here on Earth we do not have an enduring home, but we are looking forward for an everlasting home.[401]

---

399   Gen. 12:2–3
400   Eccles. 3:11
401   Heb. 13:14

Abraham had no children at the time of the covenant, and according to God, the worship would begin by a people of Abraham's descent. The situation implied that the promises of the covenant would take a combination of time and enduring faith to accomplish. I do not intend to narrate the process in detail. I want to show God's purpose in the established covenant—how the result benefits the nations of the earth. The process shows God's trustworthiness in action. God spoke of His covenant seven times to Abraham, twice to Isaac, and three times to Jacob. Abraham is the father of Isaac, and Isaac is the father of Jacob. The twelve traditional tribes of Israel are named after the twelve sons of Jacob, as each of the twelve tribes is a direct descendant of Jacob's sons.

God said to Jacob, who He named Israel in Bethel,[402]

I am God Almighty; be fruitful and increase in number. A nation and a community of nations will come from you, and kings will come from your body. The land I gave to Abraham and Isaac I also give to you, and I will give this land to your descendants after you.[403] I am the God of your fathers; do not fear to go down to Egypt for I will make you a great nation there.[404]

Accordingly, the children of Israel prospered in Egypt and became the nation that God wanted. Jacob entered the land of Egypt with his family of seventy.[405] After 430 years in Egypt, his

---

402   Gen. 32:22–28; "God said to him, 'Your name is Jacob, but you will no longer be called Jacob; your name will be Israel.' So He named him Israel" (Gen. 35:10).

403   Gen. 35:11–12

404   Gen. 46:3; the journey to Egypt was a result of famine, which besieged the entire region, except Egypt, and the discovery that Joseph, one of Jacob's sons, was then prince in Egypt.

405   Gen. 46:26–27

descendants departed the land under the leadership of Moses. They were approximately six hundred thousand men, excluding the number of women and children.[406] By the account in Exodus, chapter 1,

The children of Israel were fruitful in Egypt and increased abundantly. They multiplied and grew exceedingly mighty, and the land of Egypt was filled with them.[407]

Having suffered severe bondage by the hands of their Egyptian taskmasters, the Israelites had a great longing to depart Egypt. When He commissioned Moses to lead the people, God said,

I am the Lord. I appeared to Abraham, to Isaac and to Jacob as God almighty, but by my name, Lord I was not known to them. I have also established my covenant with them, to give them the land of Canaan, the land of their pilgrimage, in which they were strangers.[408]

The name God Almighty translates in Hebrew to *El-Shaddai.* The meanings may include "All-powerful One" and "One Who Is Sufficient."

In the burning bush,[409] God introduced Himself to Moses as I AM—the name by which He wished to be known among the

---

406   Ex. 12:37
407   Ex. 1:7
408   Ex. 6:2–4; Abraham lived in Canaan as a stranger. Isaac was born in Canaan and also his son, Jacob. Jacob and his family lived in Canaan before they went down to Egypt. In Gen. 12:7, God appeared to Abraham in Canaan and said, "To your offspring I will give this land."
409   Ex. 3

people. I AM is the name that expressed God's dependable character to earn the full trust of His people.[410] The name demonstrates the characteristic by which Abraham, Isaac, and Jacob did not experience God. Therefore, what God said to Moses does not imply that Abraham, Isaac, and Jacob did not know God and never recognized Him as Lord. The new name confirms the new level of relationship—the kind that God did not have with Abraham, Isaac, and Jacob.

God's covenant with the forefathers is based on promises of land, population, and material blessing. The population of Israel's children inherits the promise in practical terms through promising obedience, which God has made the center of delightful worship.[411] To meet the demand, Israel had to get out of Egypt. It took the strong hand of God against the Pharaoh of Egypt to let the people go.[412]

The proposed worship was commenced at the foot of Mount Sinai after the Israelites journeyed out of Egypt across the Red Sea to the desert of Sinai. They settled on the foot of Mount Sinai, which is also called Mount Horeb, and were there for about eleven months.

God asked Moses to assemble the people; He spoke to the people through Moses,

> *You have seen what I did to Egypt and how I carried you on eagles' wings and brought you to myself. Now therefore, if you will indeed obey my voice and keep my covenant, then you shall be a special treasure to me above all people; for all the earth is mine. And you shall be to me a kingdom of priests and a holy nation.*[413]

---

410   Ex. 3:13–14

411   "If you fully obey the Lord your God and carefully follow all His commands I give you today, the Lord your God will set you high above all the nations on Earth. All these blessings will come upon you and accompany you if you obey the Lord your God" (Deut. 28:1–2).

412   Ex. chapters 5–14

413   Ex. 19:4–6

God's plan for Israel is evident in His speech. When the people heard from Moses everything that God had spoken to them, they responded,

All that the Lord has spoken we will do.[414]

God's words and the people's response formed the basis of the covenant. The covenant opened the door of God's special presence in the midst of His people's gathering. The gathering in Sinai marked the beginning of conventional worship; nothing of the kind exited before then. The occasion marked the first installment of the law for the people and the sealing of the covenant with blood sacrifice.[415]

On Mount Sinai, Moses received the Ten Commandments and the instruction to construct the meeting tent, which served as center for worship. The meeting tent, or the tabernacle or sanctuary, typified God's dwelling among His people. The people were prepared in special ways to join the worship ceremony. God said to Moses,

Go to the people and consecrate them today and tomorrow and let them wash their clothes.[416]

The event of Sinai was the first direct worship encounter between God and the people. God's presence among the people confirmed His statement to Moses:

By my name Lord I did not make myself known your fathers.

Like the sound of thunder, God spoke directly to the people during the worship meeting, and Moses enlightened the people

---

414   Ex. 19:8
415   Ex. 24:4; Ex. 24:7–8
416   Ex. 19:10

concerning the rule of God's law. The congregation saw God's presence descend upon the mountain like fire:

Its smoke ascended like the smoke of a furnace, and the mountain quaked greatly. And when the blast of the trumpet sounded long and become louder and louder, Moses spoke and God answered him by voice.[417]

The event glorified the restoration of God's special presence among humanity. God first had this relationship with humankind in the Garden of Eden before the fall of Adam and Eve.

The covenant of Sinai was the beginning of a tradition of honoring and praising God through sacrifice. Moses built an altar for the Lord, and the Israelites commemorated God's presence with burnt offering. They made a peace offering by sacrificing an ox to God,[418] and Moses sealed the covenant with the animal's blood.

Unfortunately, the order did not last long. The people corrupted themselves with the golden calf, going against God's commandment that they should have no gods beside Him:

When the people saw that Moses was so long in coming down from the mountain, they gathered around Aaron and said, "Come, make us gods who will go before us. As for this fellow, Moses, who brought us up out of Egypt, we don't know what has happened to him." So Aaron answered them, "Take off the gold earrings that your wives, your sons and your daughters are wearing and bring them to me." He took what they handed him and made it into an idol cast in the shape of a calf, fashioning it with tool. They said, "These are your gods, O Israel, who

---

417   Ex. 19:18–20
418   Ex. 24: 5–6

brought you up out of Egypt." So the next day the people rose early, and sacrificed burnt offerings and presented fellowship offerings. Afterward they sat down to eat and drink and got up to indulge in festivities.[419]

Aaron was hassled to act according to the people's demand. Avoiding idol worship is among God's first four commandments to the people, which apply to all of God's children:

I am the Lord your God who brought you out of Egypt, out of the land of slavery. You shall have no other gods beside me. You shall not make for yourself an idol in the form of anything in heaven above or on the earth beneath or in the waters below. You shall not bow down to them or worship them; for I, the Lord your God, am a jealous God, punishing the children for the sin of the fathers to the third and fourth generation of those who hate me, but showing love to a thousand generations of those who love me and keep my commandments.[420]

It is regretful that, even though the Israelites had seen firsthand the invisible power of God in action—when God led them to safety through open sea and drowned Pharaoh's army and chariots that chased after them[421]—they wanted a familiar sort God, that of the

---

419   Ex. 32:1–5

420   Ex. 20:2–4

421   Ex. 14: 21–23; "Then Moses stretched out his hand over the sea, and all that night the Lord drove the sea back with a strong east wind and turned it into dry land. The waters were divided, and the Israelites went through the sea on dry land. The Egyptians pursued them, and all Pharaoh's horses and chariots and horsemen followed them into the sea. Then the Lord said to Moses, 'Stretch out your hand over the sea so that the waters may flow back over the Egyptians and their chariots and horsemen'" (Ex. 14:26).

Egyptians, which they could see and shape into whatever image pleased them. Because of their unfaithfulness, God elected among the people the tribe of Levi to be priests on behalf of the entire nation. With the coming of Jesus Christ, Son of David, God extended the privilege of priesthood yet again to all believers.

The story of the Israelites as they traveled through the wilderness en route to the Promised Land is a testimonial event. Each of the steps shows how God demonstrates His judgment and salvation before human error. Reference to the journey of the Israelites in prayer consolidates believers' call for God's deliverance and care, especially in times of great need. The psalmist prayed for God's deliverance with reference to His mercy, which enabled the people to inherit the land:

> *We have heard with our ears, O God. Our fathers have told us what you did in their days, in days long ago. With Your hand, you drove out the nations and planted our fathers. You crushed the people and made our father flourish. It was not by their sword that they won over the land, nor did their arm bring them victory. It was your right hand; your arm, and the light of your face, for you love them.*[422]

Israel: The Endurance of Our Salvation

God acts in all human history, even when human beings are not aware of His presence and purpose. The election of Israel is, according to biblical witness, an expression of the mystery of God's way. We may not be able to explain why God's revelation came when it did and where it did. From Israel's prophets is no evidence that Israel is more religiously discerning and better than other peoples of the world. According to the book of Deuteronomy, God's choice of Israel

---

422   Ps. 44: 1–3

was a free act of grace bestowed for the sake of humanity without consideration of the worth of its object:

It is not because of your righteousness or your integrity that you are going to take possession of their land; but on account of the wickedness of these nations. The Lord your God will drive them out before you, to accomplish what He swore to your fathers; to Abraham, Isaac, and Jacob. Understand, then, that it is not because of your righteousness that the Lord your God is giving you this good land to possess, for you are stiff-necked people.[423]

God freed the nation of Israel from slavery in Egypt as an expression of sovereign freedom and unmerited love.

As a matter of fact, if we were to give other reasons for God's election of Israel, we would make God's action conditional, thereby reducing it to something less than an expression of divine freedom and grace. It is biblical witness that God manifests His sovereignty over the whole world through the history of this particular people. The evidence in history connects great national suffering by the hands of wickedness; also to the Christian Church, the inheritor of the promise to Abraham.

The scripture foresaw that God would justify the Gentiles by faith and announced the Gospel in advance to Abraham. "All nations will be blessed through you." So those who have faith are blessed along with Abraham, the man of faith.[424]

In all things, a true belief endures much painful sacrifice to reach its righteous end. Long and bitter suffering in Egypt did not

---

423   Deut. 9:5–6
424   Gal. 3:8–9

indicate any real hindrance to Israel's hope for God's deliverance. The people were held together by their spiritual strength. Their spirits fed on God's promise, and thereby, they kept every hope alive until God's time arrived.

Any evil that defeats you through the force of pain must first capture your spiritual strength. Facing daily struggle by means of spiritual strength means that we must focus on God's word, which counters frustration and pain. Faith does not fail if the purpose aligns with God's plan.

Four generations of Israel's children were wasted in bondage before God's time to set the people freed arrived, but their sacrifice was not in vain. As part of the process of salvation, the people suffered for faith and led their young generation to the appointed time. Like all suffering in life that is associated with faith, the suffering of the Israelites allowed them, by steadfastness, to finally achieve the purpose that God allowed for. God is not responsible for the Israelite's suffering; human wickedness was.

Even so, God's judgment takes every action into account. God decided that Israel would be temporally placed out of Canaan, away from the fornications of the Canaanites on the land. The Canaanites' religious ceremonies were based on fertility of cults and honored many different gods. Egypt offered an ideal refuge for the sons of Jacob—a home for the nation that God proposed to Abraham, a nation of one ancestral blood.[425]

By revelation, Abraham understood what would happen before it was made manifest:

Know for certain that your descendants will be strangers in a country not their own, and they will be enslaved and mistreated

---

425   Gen. 12:2–3; Gen. 15:1–6; Gen. 46:2–4; to Jacob is the affirmation of God's promise to Abraham.

four hundred years. But I will punish the nation they serve as slaves, and afterward they will come out with great possessions. You, however, will go to your fathers in peace and be buried at a good old age. In the fourth generation your descendants will come back here, for the sins of the Amorites has not yet reached its full measure.[426]

Outside the biblical claim, God's promise of a nation could be vague by any logical standards if Jacob's children had stayed in Canaan and multiplied with the pagan communities. The children of Israel would corrupt themselves by pagan marriage, which would result in mixing of blood amid idol worship. Direct links to Abraham's lineage would probably disappear and God's promise of a nation would be looked upon by critics as coincidental and biologically ordinary. For a second time, God took drastic measures to safeguard His purpose. When the children of Israel were about to enter the land, God instructed them,

In the cities of the nations the Lord is giving you as an inheritance, do not leave alive anything that breathes. Completely destroy them—the Hittites, Amorites, Canaanites, Perizzites, Hivites, and Jebusites—as the Lord your God has commanded you. Otherwise, they will teach you to follow all the detestable things they do in worshiping their gods, and you will sin against the Lord your God.[427]

The land of the Canaanites, defined as including these tribes, was deemed suitable for conquest on moral grounds. Maintaining the Israelites as one people is a particular reference in history that is

---

426   Gen. 15:12–16
427   Deut. 20:16–18

necessary to bring about God's plan. Having been chosen by grace and fortified by righteousness Israel is set apart as the flag bearer of the gift of Jesus Christ, son of David.

The fullness of the Gospel takes pleasure in the spiritual origin of the law. In both the Old and the New Testaments, God's salvation is the central theme of the Bible, and Jesus Christ is the center of history. His presence profoundly reveals the meaning of the entire historical theological process and divides the age into two—the age before and the age after His death and resurrection. The New Testament writing closed where it does because the Church bears witness to faith that God has spoken and acted once and for all.

> *For Christ died for sins once for all, the righteous for the unrighteous, to bring you to God. He was put to death in the body but made alive by the Spirit, through whom also He went and preached to the spirits in prison who disobeyed long ago when God waited patiently in the days of Noah while the ark was being built. In it only a few people, eight in all, were saved through water, and this water symbolizes baptism that now saves you also—not the removal of dirt from the body but the pledge of a good conscience toward God.*[428]

Jesus' fate on the cross again illustrates the significance of endurance to our salvation. The earliest missionaries bear the mark of much pain as a result of the troubles of their time, especially in defense of God's goodness. Our time has its fair share of challenges, and endurance is a significant part of our strategy for survival. Pain is

---

428   1 Peter 3:18–22; "The spirit in prison" seems to imply those who died with no true idea of the living God. They disobeyed in ignorance and died in sin. In three days before resurrecting from the dead, Jesus ministered to those spirits that they too may hear the Gospel and decide whether to be saved.

the physiological cause of many experiences of suffering. The reality that so much suffering exists is still a mystery to secular mind and poses moral problems for many believers. Things that work against God's will in our lives exist around us, but we are kept safe through patience, persistent faith, and prayer.

Righteous suffering will be rewarded, but hope does not take away all the pain of suffering, especially as wickedness multiplies. Perseverance warrants that everyone must be mentally and spiritually strong. Pain is a key hindrance to happiness, and sometimes walking with God requires the cost of our comfort. Backslide indicates lack of endurance; Christians who fall back from faith are usually less adapted to suffering. Either worldliness or frustration could block our sight of the goal when we lack the spiritual strength to endure beyond the present hardship.

Spiritual strength is particularly more able to support faith in difficult times, and all God's children should adopt an enduring spirit to be particularly strong. Weakness of spirit is the worst form of weakness and constitutes part of a person's unrighteousness.

Ungodliness sets the path of evil upon the world; accordingly, evil controls the world through pain. But the pain of evil is sidelined when Jesus Christ takes the center stage of a person's life. Judgment by the enemy is temporal, but peace of the Lord is everlasting. Jesus said,

My friends do not be afraid of those who kill the body and after that have no more that they can do. But I will show you whom you should fear: Fear Him who, after He has killed, has the power to cast into hell.[429]

God is the reason to face life without fear.

---

429   Luke 12: 4–5; judgment by our enemies is merely physical and temporal, but God's judgment has an everlasting consequence.

The Faith of Two Covenants

Rather than *covenant*, we are more familiar with *testament* as the titles of two major sections of the Bible. The Bible is a book of two major covenants—the old and the new covenants. The Old Testament theme runs through the covenant of Sinai and marks the history of Israel as a people of God. The New Testament theme reveals the joy of the blood covenant sealed on the cross of Calvary for all humanity.

The new covenant gathers up hope for the final salvation and brings to fulfillment the spiritual history of Israel. The basic framework of the new covenant is eschatology; it addresses the time when God will gather the saints and bring this age to an end. The old covenant believers were also eschatological by expecting the Messiah who would step into history and usher in the new age. The old covenant viewed Jesus Christ as the Messiah by anticipation; the new covenant confirms Him the Immanuel.[430]

The Holy Spirit is responsible for the geographical expansion of the house and people of God, which in no way contradicts the oneness of the Godhead and the uniqueness of all God's children. We must tell God's truth from the dimension of its spiritual origin. The outpouring of God's Spirit represents a unique relevance; in no such way is God revealed to humanity throughout the setting of history. God centered every important thing about worship on salvation, which His Son brought to the world. God is forever committed to honoring humanity's sacrifice and praise offered in His Son's name. His Holy Spirit inspires the oneness of worship, as it should be between Jews and Gentiles. Whoever accepts the good news must tell of its joy without mixing it with other ideas.

Christianity in particular is a faith without passport and visa. The Christian Church should have no barriers of nationality, race, and social standing. Christ breaks down all barriers and accepts all

---

430   Isa. 7:14; Matt. 1:23

people who come to Him. By grace, God seeks to rescue the world from sin and nothing should keep us from telling people about Christ or accepting into our fellowship any and all believers of the living God. Worshippers of the living God should build bridges, not walls. Even the apostles were astonished to witness the gift of the Holy Spirit poured out on Gentiles when they heard the Gentiles speaking in tongues and praising God.[431]

> For He Himself is our peace, who has made two one and has destroyed the barrier; the dividing wall of hostility.[432]

In response, the world requires oneness of faith to be free from all guilt, and members of God's family should pursue holiness as one goal for all. Paul offered a strategy to help us live up to the expectation:

> Therefore, as God's chosen people, holy and dearly loved, clothe yourselves with compassion, kindness, humility, gentleness, and patience. Bear with each other and forgive whatever grievances you may have against one another. Forgive as the Lord forgives you, and over all these virtues put on love, which binds them together in perfect unity. Let the peace of Christ rule in your hearts, since as members of one body you are called to peace. Be thankful. Let the word of Christ dwell in you richly as you teach and admonish one another with all wisdom, and as you sing psalms, hymns, and spiritual songs with gratitude in your hearts to God. And whatever you do, whether in word or deed, do it all in the name of the Lord Jesus, giving thanks to God the Father through Him.[433]

---

431   Acts 10:45–46
432   Eph. 2:14
433   Col. 3:12–17

Jesus Christ is the incarnation of God the Father. His Church engages one fellowship between the godhead and believers. The Church serves as an extension of the incarnation—the body of Christ. The Holy Spirit dwells in the Son, and through the Son, everyone, by virtue of His work of redemption, is God's child. The identity is one Church, one soul, and one pastor.

Covenant is no ordinary relationship; it is a relationship entered into by decision—one in which there is an inward and spontaneous acknowledgment of God's sovereignty over all of life. No new covenant was formed when the Church split into East and West. No new covenant was formed during or after the Protestant Reformation, and no new covenant was formed by modern-day Judaism.

Jesus Christ is the only high priest of God's worship; the assignment to preach God's kingdom came from no one else but His Spirit. His sign, gift of the Spirit, belongs to all people and serves the good of all people.

For just as Moses lifted up the snake in the desert, so the son of man must be lifted up that everyone who believes in Him may have eternal life.[434]

The Bible has a focal point in this verse, showing the covenants as neither static nor self-centered. It is God's will that whoever calls on the name of the Lord Jesus Christ will be saved.[435] The biblical God does not speak to humanity from an ivory tower above the rough-and-tumble of ordinary life. He reveals Himself in the concrete places where men live. If our convention and worship is thin, it is not so by God's making. We slip because we ignore the essence of delightful worship. Every moment of crisis is a moment

---

434   John 3:14
435   Rom. 10:13

of truth and tough decision making. Ironically, division generates diminishing trust, and every worship leader could be potentially suspect.

Another key connection to the covenants is the concept of consecration. In Exodus, chapter 24, God instructed the children of Israel to prepare to meet with His presence. They were consecrated, and they washed their clothes.[436] Referring to chapter 4 of this book, Christians borrowed the concept and wear dressy clothes for the Sunday morning worship.

Using the Old Testament theme, consecration takes place through rituals and prayer. The elaborate system of specifications found in the book of Leviticus describing how a person could be clean was designed to promote physical cleanliness and continual recognition of God in all ways of life. The people relied on an annual ceremony of leading a scapegoat into the desert or a solitary land to bear away the nation's sin.[437] Sprinkling of holy water was occasioned as means to authenticate bodily cleansing. Water was made holy by praying over it.

According to Hebrews, chapter 9, the imagery of the Day of Atonement[438] prefigured Jesus Christ:

For this is an illustration for the present time, indicating that the gifts and sacrifices being offered were not able to clean the conscience of the worshipper. They are only a matter of food and drink and various ceremonial washings—external regulations applying until the time of the new order. When Christ came as High Priest of the good things that are already here; He went through a greater and more perfect tabernacle that is not man-made; that is, not of this creation. He did not enter by means of

---

436   Ex. 19: 10–11
437   Lev. 16:10
438   Lev. 16

the blood of goats and calves, but by His own blood He entered the Most Holy Place once for all.[439]

Under the new covenant, a proper devotion can be regarded as consecration, not necessarily the symbolic sprinkling of holy water and the burning of incense. If the blood of bulls and goats, the ashes of a heifer, and the sprinkling of the unclean with blessed water can sanctify body and soul, how cannot the blood of Jesus Christ do more? He, who, through the eternal Spirit offered Himself without spot to God, cleanses our conscience from acts, which leads to spiritual dead that we may serve the living God in truth and in Spirit.[440]

By both the old and the new covenants, consecration resonates one meaning within the spiritual context, which is sanctity. The instruction, "consecrate them and let them wash their clothes" suggests a spiritual exercise of excusing the body from lust and the heart from sinful thoughts, which rebel against God's presence.

I am the Lord your God, you shall therefore consecrate yourselves; and you shall be holy; for I am holy.[441]

God's holiness motivates Christian holiness. When committed to holiness, you will live by the rule of God's presence. A devoted believer watches over himself to keep his mind clean and ready to work with God. It is impossible to achieve perfection from the slips of this earthly life, but the practice of holiness makes near perfection very possible.

---

439   Heb. 9:9–12

440   "For this reason, Jesus Christ is the mediator of a new covenant, that those who are called may receive the promised eternal inheritance now that He has died as a ransom to set free from the sins committed under the first covenant" (Heb. 9:13–15).

441   Lev. 11:44

The commemorated worship blessing of Exodus, chapter 24, is, through Jesus Christ, extended to all believers. The blessing of Abraham has its profoundness in Jesus Christ, son of David and Messiah of all people. As His coming brought the old covenant to fulfillment, Jesus reveals the full dimension of the new covenant with spiritual worship. No further tension should exist between personal and institutional worship.

Israel was on the move in the wilderness when God told Moses to construct a tent for His presence. The pattern of the tent in its measurements—length, size, and material structure—came from God. God said to Moses,

Moreover you shall make the Tabernacle with ten curtains of fine woven linen, and blue, purple, and scarlet thread; with artistic designs of Cherubim you shall weave them. The length of each curtain shall be twenty-eight cubits and the width of the curtains shall have the same measurements.[442]

Moses followed the blueprint and made the portable shelter. The priests carried ahead of the people the tent and Ark of the Covenant, which contained the stone tablets, Aaron's staff that budded, and a golden jar of manna.[443] The meeting tent served as a place of worship from that point until the time the people entered the land. Joshua finally pitched the tent in Shiloh.[444]

King David institutionalized national worship in Jerusalem and made material arrangements for the magnificent temple that his son,

---

442   Ex. 26:1–2; Exodus, chapters 25 through 31 cover the entire specifications of the tabernacle in the way that God described it to Moses.

443   Heb. 9:4

444   "Now the whole congregation of the Children of Israel assembled together at Shiloh, and set up the Tabernacle of meeting there" (Josh. 18:1).

King Solomon, built. King Solomon dedicated the new temple to serve global convention—as a place of prayer for all nations:

> *Concerning a foreigner, who is not of your people Israel, but has come from a far country for your name's sake—for they too will hear of your great name and your strong hand and outstretched arm—when he comes and prays toward this temple. Then hear from heaven, your dwelling place, and do whatever the foreigner asks of you, so that all the peoples of the earth may know your name and fear you.*[445]

Conventional worship had taken place in houses made of brick ever since the people settled on the land. Three important factors emerged from the blueprint of the tent. First, the later temples were built upon the pattern. Second, temple worship became the center of the Jewish national life, essentially because worship was the most significant item in the parcel of blessing. Third, the tent is of divine origin and an immensely important representation of God's idea of worship impressed upon the world. Its special meaning is the likeness of the heavenly ideal to come.

> *Christ come as High Priest of the good things to come, with the greater and more perfect Tabernacle not made with hands; that is, not of this creation.*[446]

Jesus paid homage to the temple in Jerusalem in celebration of God's dwelling among men; while He did not set out the exact day of His return, He will bring with Him the heavenly ideal tabernacle.

---

445   1 King 8:41–42
446   Heb. 9:11, Heb. 9–10

It was by faith that Abraham obeyed God when he was called to go out to the place, which he would receive as an inheritance, and he went, but not knowing where he was going. By faith he lived in the land of promise as in a foreign country; he lived in tents as did Isaac and Jacob, the heirs with him of the same promise. For he waited for the city which has foundation, whose architect and builder is God.[447]

Therefore, we also since we are surrounded by so great a cloud of witness let us lay off every weight and the sin, which so easily entangles, and let us run with endurance the race that is set before us, looking unto Jesus, the author and finisher of our faith, who for the joy set before Him endured the cross despite the shame, and sat down at the right hand of the throne of God.[448]

---

447   Heb. 11:8–10
448   Heb. 12:1–2

Chapter 7

⌒✎⌒

Passing on the Blessing

I t is fundamental to know that the universe exists because of God's approval. Those who trust in the Lord live and grow by faith; each day brings in them God's new strength. Abraham was not a model of goodness at the time he took the first step of faith and answered God's call. He learned to improve his behavior and thereby become the faithful one.[449]

True faith results in deed and culminates in righteousness. Faith in the right kind of life is the basis of justification, which indicates that a person is justified by what he or she does and not by faith alone. Like Abraham, each believer has started the race somewhere; those who uphold the work of righteousness through faith shall make better their behavior in the same way that partnership with Jesus Christ is a life-changing experience.

Jesus Christ is the rock of our salvation. On His account, we all base our journey of faith. You are special by surrendering your life and worries to His care. The Bible defines God's people as

---

449   James 2:23–24; Gen. 15:6; Rom. 4:3; Gal. 3:6

the apple of His eye.[450] And whatever touches them also touches God.

> *For the Lord has done this and it is marvelous in our eyes that each day is a day made by the Lord; therefore let us rejoice and be glad on it.*[451]

Some believers think of themselves as lowly in self-pity, despite timeless hope in God. Such an attitude does not provide the foundation on which we may live the full experience of God's blessing. Having a gloomy view of your image is not humility. Being downcast about oneself denies God's love. Negative self-perception results from personal guilt and indifferent attitude in our society. Accordingly, everyone makes progress in God; even the unfaithful feel the repercussion of their unfaithfulness.

But the strength of faith is obtained by the knowledge that everyone's weakness has a place in the strength of Christ's grace. We are motivated by the prospect of embracing fully the blessings of God. Those who do not know that they will finally be saved by believing God are usually not saved at first.

I trust in God, and He guides me through the wondrous works of His mercies. I dare not claim righteousness as a result of my belief, yet my trust in an inherited grace is not hypocrisy. By faith, Abraham passed on God's blessing to his descendants—not as a tribute to righteousness but to the continuing love of God. Jesus Christ bears the blessing that benefits all people. If Abraham could gain favor from God without any claim of merit but by faith and good work, the rest of humanity should harvest in Jesus Christ the same claim.

---

450   Zech. 2:8; Ps. 116:15
451   Ps. 118:23–24

The Pentecost gave birth to the Church's blessing[452] as an ever-widening circle; it is the source of the gift that cultivates the Gospel. The Pentecost answered the prophecy by Joel as the beginning of the last days:

> *It shall come to pass afterwards that I will pour out My Spirit on all flesh, and also on my menservants and on my maidservants. And it shall come to pass that whoever calls on the name of the Lord shall be saved.*[453]

The outpouring of God's Spirit has a unique relevance; it will reach the final point with Jesus' second coming. Joel's prophecy and the actual fulfillment on the Pentecost day signify that now is the prolonged last days. We may interpret the rising of violence that characterizes contemporary history as the beckoning of God. Our problem as blessed people is that harvest cannot take place where no seed is sown.[454] You have the power to sow the seed; therefore, use it.

God is less glorified when we do not help the world in darkness to embrace the light of His call. Jesus said,

> *I have set you an example that you should do as I have done for you. I tell you the truth, no servant is greater than his master is, neither is a messenger greater than the one who sent him.*

---

452   Deut. 16:16; Lev. 23:15–16; Pentecost is an annual Jewish festival, also known as the Festival of the Weeks or the day of First Fruits; it is a celebration of the first buds of the harvest. Jewish law requires Jewish men to go to Jerusalem at least three times in a year to celebrate major feasts—Passover, Pentecost, and the feast of the Tabernacles.

453   Joel 2:28–32

454   Acts 1:8, Jesus said, "For you will receive power when the Holy Spirit comes upon you; and you will be my witness in Jerusalem, and in all Judea, and Samaria, to the end of the earth."

Now that you know these things, you will be blessed if you do them.[455]

When God said to Adam and Eve, "Go and multiple, be fruitful, and fill the earth," He meant that the earth would desire godliness. The task of the Christian commission[456] is to help the Holy Spirit complete the work of revival. There is no revival outside God; and the blessing of the Holy Spirit works by individual response.

The work of being a special blessing to people is neither complex nor impractical.

He who refreshes others will himself be refreshed.[457]

Jesus invites you personally to bear the burden of His witness. If God's salvation could be timely gained, why postpone your resolution? Spread the good news of His precious love that the world in sin may repent, obtain pardon, and free from the guilt of sin. The person you will be at your time of death begins with what you make of yourself today. Do not imagine overcoming all hindrance in one day. You are blessed if you engage the works of righteousness to revive people, which is a gateway for people to escape God's wrath. Confidence to die is confidence gained while living.

---

455   John 13:15–17

456   "All authority in heaven and on Earth has been given to me. Therefore, go and make disciples of all nations, baptizing them in the name of the Father and of the Son and of the Holy Spirit, and teaching them to obey everything I have commanded you. And surely I am with you always to the very end of the age" (Matt. 28:18–20).

457   Prov. 11: 25

The Spirit Unites

The next step after accepting Jesus Christ is to embrace the Church. This step includes confessing your new relationship to friends and families. You might be the chosen one through whom your family and friends could become part of the blessing. Always seek opportunity to share publicly your experience of the Lord. If possible, invite your contacts to Church and engage them in discussion about the Bible often. Let people around you be familiar with your constant talk about God's goodness. You will gain from enjoying the Holy Spirit's presence with everybody.

God's salvation forms the basis for everyday relationships and expands your blessing to benefit as many people as you can relate to. The Holy Spirit provides in you the corridor of opportunity through which every available person could be reached and be saved. Your input to God's work is part of the true character of love, which is the way to God. Prophet Joel said,

Tell your children about it; let your children tell their children and their children to another generation.[458]

Joel proclaimed discipleship as a rallying point of the Holy Spirit's influence, which implies using the authority in the word for outreach. Jesus' ministry is done in the proclaimed power of the Holy Spirit,[459] by which we are part of His ministry. Every believer is connected to the ministry; the word *disciple* is not assigned to only those gifted to work miracles and those who start and oversee

---

458   Joel 1:3

459   "The Spirit of the Lord is upon me; He has anointed me to preach the Gospel to the poor. He has sent me to heal the brokenhearted, to proclaim liberty to the captives, and recover the sight of the blind, to set at liberty those who are oppressed and to proclaim the acceptance year of the Lord" (Luke 4:18–19).

Churches. Every believer is light and ought to shine. God's word is the seed of His kingdom. Those who speak His word in blessing are sowing with profound interest in people's souls. It is through the seed of God's kingdom that a soul can be born into the kingdom.[460]

Speaking of blessing highlights the importance of evangelism with regard to the power of spoken word. Spoken word is not cheap, as some people assume it is. David said,

Keep your tongue from evil and your lips from speaking deceit.[461]

The goodness of word is the awareness of its engaging promises; otherwise the Gospel could serve as a hammer, especially in the hands of those who use the Gospel for personal judgment. The word we speak has its profound origin in God; and the manner in which we speak can have either positive or adverse effects. The command of word emerged from God's heart.

God's spoken word is the mysterious power responsible for the creation.

God said, "Let there be light" and there was light. God saw that the light was good and He separated the light from darkness.[462] *Then He said, "Let us make man in our image, in our likeness.*[463]

---

460   Matt. 4: 4 "Man shall not live by bread alone, but by every word that proceeds out of the mouth of God."

461   Ps. 34: 13

462   Gen. 1: 3 - 4

463   Gen. 1: 26, God spoke as the creator King when He announced His work to the angels in heaven. His heavenly throne surrounded by the angelic members of His court is revealed in 1kings 22: 19 where prophet Micaiah said, "Therefore hear the word of the Lord: I saw the Lord sitting on His throne with all the host of heaven standing around Him on His right and on His left."

So God proceeded to create man in His image; male and female He made them.

Spoken word formed the blessing that God gave to Abraham. Abraham inherited the land that belonged to Canaan because God agreed to it. Noah blessed Shem and cursed Ham; Shem's descendants prospered because of this blessing while the generations of Ham were denied their heritage.[464]

The spoken word of Isaac formed the blessing that his son, Jacob, denied his brother, Esau. Esau bitterly wept and practically mourned himself when he heard Isaac's blessing to Jacob.[465] The effect of Isaac's word is gain to Jacob's descendants.[466] The sons of Esau were the only neighbors of Israel that never gained from God any promise of mercy.[467] Jacob's blessings, like the force of the Spirit, shaped the lives of his descendents.[468]

Nothing will ever replace spoken word as the mainstream of the Gospel. On account of Jesus Christ, every believer will forever

---

464 "Noah, a man of the soil, proceeded to plant a vineyard. When he drank some of its wine, he became drunk and lay uncovered inside his tent. Ham, the father of Canaan, saw his father's nakedness and told his two brothers outside. But Shem and Japheth took a garment and laid it across their shoulders; then they walked in backward and covered their father's nakedness. Their faces were turned the other way so that they would not see their father's nakedness. When Noah woke from his wine and found out what his youngest son had done to him, he said, 'Cursed be Canaan. The lowest of slaves will he be to his brothers.' He also said, 'Blessed be the Lord, the God of Shem! May Canaan be the slave of Shem, may God extend the territory of Japheth, may Japheth live in the tents of Shem, and may Canaan be his slave.'" (Gen. 9:20–27).

465 "When Esau heard his father's verdict, he burst out with a loud and bitter cry, and he said to his father, 'Bless me—me too, my father!'" (Gen. 27:34).

466 Gen. 36: 1

467 Isa. 34:5–6 ; Isa. 63:1

468 Gen. 27

reap the fruits of the blessing; God has spoken it. The Passover feast took a new meaning from Jesus' word and became the celebration of universal salvation. By the power of His word, Jesus made the Last Supper the central act of Christian worship. He used the bread and wine of the supper as visual aids to explain the meaning of His coming to die. The bread the twelve disciples ate represented His body and the wine His blood; therefore, the reality of their connection to His death is beyond doubt. Jesus established the everlasting usefulness of this ceremony by telling all generations of His disciples to repeat the ceremony in worship occasions. His word over the cup made the point obvious:

This cup is the new covenant in my blood; do this, whenever you drink it, in memory of me.[469]
This is my blood of the new covenant, which is poured out for many for the forgiveness of sins.[470]

The Passover feast, by the new concept, will finally celebrate the ultimate union of saints:

They shall have no more need for every man to teach his neighbor, or a man his brother saying, "Know the Lord." For they all shall know me. From the least of them to the greatest of them and I, the Lord, will forgive their sin and will remember their iniquities no more.[471]

The engagement does not only remind participants of the redemptive sacrifice of Christ but anticipates when the memorial supper will give way to the messianic banquet. By the assurance of

469   1 Cor. 11: 25
470   Matt. 26: 28
471   Jer. 31: 34

His word, we look forward beyond Jesus' imminent death to what the meal will achieve. To bless is to connect people to spiritual prosperity; the reason to speak of blessing in prayer is to gain spiritual prosperity. The role of an evangelist is to use the power of words to favor people. We must desire to bless and should apply the power of word with an attitude of love and in friendliness. We owe one another the encouragement to experience godliness. To understand the depth of God's love for humanity, first consider God's love for His Son whom He gave to die for humanity's sake. Jesus said,

You did not choose me; I chose you.[472]

What Difference Can I Make?

The Holy Spirit provides support so that we can evangelize the world; and part of the support is the spiritual gift. God is not impressed that you possess one or more gift. He is impressed when you submit to His will and willfully allow the Spirit to use and strengthen you for His purpose. Your spiritual gift can be like a car saved in a garage (the car is protected but not in use) or like food preserved in a refrigerator (the food is safe but less useful than if you were to eat it). Like birthday cake, each small piece of your gift brings great joy and many good wishes. Your role in making disciples is to help people reinvest in the love and power that God invested in you. As it is said, the only thing you could possibly take from this life to meet with God in heaven is saved souls. Your ability to present Jesus Christ to people suggests your spiritual usefulness to them. Your duty is to play your role in life well; the results are up to the Holy Spirit. It may take years before a preached message or help toward repentance gets into a person.

In helping a new convert grow in faith, you must spend time with the convert. Make a habit of visiting with the new convert as

---

472   John 15: 16

frequently as is necessary to keep the new relationship alive. Take precautions to ensure that the time spent with new converts concerns the Bible. The aim is not only to sell the Gospel but to equip a new convert steadily with faith until he or she can fully withstand the truth and stand by his or her understanding strongly enough to teach other people. God directs His anointed ones to regularly measure steps alongside goals. Paul guided his step alongside his missionary goal by exerting himself to the utmost. He returned to the field to measure growth, and he never took his eyes off the Churches that he planted. He wrote letters while in prison; some of the Churches received guidance to counter their mistakes while he encouraged all progress made in the Lord. The significance of measuring growth is that doing so allows you to develop better ways and techniques most suitable for the task within any environment. With reference to time and place, we must take every step of growth seriously. It was not all the Jews delivered out of Egypt who made it to the Promised Land. The temptation that caused a majority of the Jews to fail in the desert is literally the same lust that constitutes a major part of modern-day struggles. Even when working within your local environment, you ought to let your program grow out of the setting. The tactic uses every available means to reach every available person. The purpose of salvation is not religion but the process of what God has done to reconcile everyone to Himself. Begin your witness by communicating the message well; this should create understanding for prospective converts and lead them to acceptance, involvement, and spiritual growth. Communication is primarily verbal and should be on the level of the person's understanding. Nothing else comes before the call to help a person understand the purpose of salvation until the person is saved. When engaging someone in conversation, you must prepare to share part of your story. Through your openness—through sharing your life's testimony with people—you will win their trust. Salvation is voluntary; it does not come to pass by words of command. To have an intimate conversation with people you evangelize is to discover the level at which they understand God's word. There is no uniformity to spirituality. Faith is limitless, and every individual reacts differently to the problem of faith. Some people need to be converted into the faith, having not accepted Jesus Christ as Lord and personal savior. Other people need revival, having fallen back from faith. You must be careful not to mismanage both circumstances; otherwise the outcome may not be what you have in mind. A person's problem with the Gospel may not be the ordinary ignorance of God's word. Many people are angry because of life's circumstance. We do not deny hardship and injustice that add difficulty to belief. Using the network of evil, Satan creates unhealthy situations to easily lure people to reject dependence upon God. Therefore, a backslider who doubts God's love does not need conversion but the assurance of Christ's redemption. Biblical counsel provides for the occasion and uplifts the spirit to consider ugly circumstance through spiritual wisdom. When sharing the Gospel, endeavor to start where a person's concern is focused and show how God's word applies to all concern. Trials and tests of faith can bring people closer to God in the same way that they can push people away from God. The implication of this, points directly to the reason you should not begin any conversation about the Gospel by asking your contact lots of question; if you do so, you may be invading someone's privacy. Multiple questions can easily upset a person and cause him or her to discontinue the conversation. In addition, do not fault the mission by assuming that all nonmembers of your brand of Church are unbelievers. Making converts is not enough; the process ends with making disciples. As it is said, middle age is not the end of growth; in adulthood, we can find daily inspiration. The work of encountering people for Jesus Christ can be more satisfying if you desire a person's future above his or her present personality. It is encouraging to fight for what a person can be in Christ, regardless of his or her present condition. The letter of the apostle Paul to Philemon is a good example of this principle. The letter tells how one can fruitfully work out a future in Jesus Christ against a sinful past. The letter contains the story about a young man, Onesimus, who was slave to a wealthy businessman, Philemon. Onesimus ran away from Philemon's house in Colossi because he was alleged of stealing Philemon's money, which under the Roman law was punishable by death. Onisemus met with Paul in Rome where Paul persuaded him through the Gospel, and he became a Christian. Paul was the apostle to Colossi and friend of Philemon. As an apostle, Paul had the authority to tell Philemon what to do, but he chose to appeal in Christian love rather than using words of command. With his letter to Philemon, Paul asked Philemon's compassion toward Onesimus. Paul said,

Perhaps the reason he was separated from you for a while was that you might have him back for good—no longer as slave, but better than a slave, as a dear brother. He is very dear to me but even dearer to you, both as a man and as a brother in the Lord.[473]

Paul testified to Onesimus' transformation and his new life, asking that Onesimus be reconciled to Philemon. Paul placed no emphasis on the type of person Onesimus was; rather he focused on who Onesimus has become. Paul's ability to convince Philemon to forgive his slave is the hand of God tearing down personal obstacles—objects that literally separate people from each other. Life-changing truth forms the backdrop of other letters from Paul. We read,

Here there is no Greeks or Jews, circumcised or uncircumcised, barbarian, Scythians, free or slaves, but Christ is all, and is in all.[474]

---

473   Philem. 15–16
474   Col. 3: 11

The Bible gave no hint to how Philemon received Onesimus, but tradition gives reasons to believe that Philemon received his former servant well and granted his liberty. Jesus Christ unites all people in God. The Gospel can change any unjust social structure by changing people within the structure. The Spirit of Christ entered Onesimus and made him recognize the social habit of his day. He went back to his master, determined to be of good behavior. The Spirit also convinced Philemon to accept Onesimus as a brother and fellow Christian. To God be the glory; Onesimus later became a bishop in Berea. In writing to Philemon, Paul must have looked back to himself—to the person he was as Saul—and considered Onesimus with great love. Paul's persuasiveness allowed Philemon no option other than the outcome.[475] In certain cases, it may not take the faith of the person in difficulty to save him or her. Your strong faith and determination can change people's life and help them get over their difficulty. The power of faith cannot be exaggerated; with faith, nothing is impossible. Jesus said,

If you have faith as small as a mustard seed, you can say to this mountain, "Move from here to there," and it will move. Nothing will be impossible for you.[476]

In other words, God's resolve will be your lead. From the same perspective, the Bible tells of a healing that Jesus Christ performed in Capernaum. Four men carried a paralytic man to the rooftop of the house where Jesus stayed because the force of the crowd waiting to meet with Jesus blocked the entrance. Jesus healed the paralytic man

---

"So if you consider me a partner, welcome him as you would welcome me. If he has done you any wrong or owe you anything, charge it to me. I, Paul, am writing this letter with my own hand. I will pay it back—not to mention that you owe me your very self" (Philem. 17–18).

476 Matt. 17: 20; "Mountain" figuratively applies to life's obstacles.

and commended the faith of the four men who broke in through the rooftop.[477] The faith of the four men was an evangelistic faith, by which the sick man was healed. The men's persistence demonstrates their strong faith in God's saving power. The sick man, in his misery, may have given up hope, but his friends would not. A more challenging problem to your task is the ability to pass on God's blessing through your own faith and determination. Your faith is the boldness of the truth. As a believer, you possess a great treasure; your faith is an open door to miracles and a gateway to favor the faithless. The prayer of the faithful asks according to God's character and will; in other words,

With faith, you may ask for whatever you want from God and it shall be granted unto you.[478]

On a different occasion in Jerusalem, Jesus met a paralyzed man by the pool called Bethesda. The man had been an invalid for thirty-eight years and sought after spiritual healing by the pool. A great number of disabled people used to lie by the pool. The Spirit of God, on occasion, stirred the water and whoever entered the pool first after the water was stirred was cured from whatever sickness he had. When Jesus came by the man, He asked the paralyzed man whether he would like to be made well. The man answered,

Sir, I have no one to help me into the pool when the water is stirred. While I am trying to get in, someone else goes down ahead of me.[479]

---

477   Mark 2:1–12
478   "Whatever you ask in my name, that I will do, that the Father may be glorified in the Son. If you ask anything in my name, I will do it" (John 14: 13–14).
479   John 5:1–15

The sick man simply explained that it was not the sickness but lack of help that had kept him by the pool for all those years. Realizing that the sick man had spent time by the pool, Jesus healed him. For thirty-eight years the man had kept alive his faith that someone eventually would help him to reach God's help. If the man had died by the pool, the real cause of his death would have been lack of help and not his disease. Ordinarily, it is easier for an afflicted person to accept his or her condition as hopeless if the afflicted has struggled with the same problem over a long period of time. But here was an exception. Suffering tends to discourage hope if the troubled person has poor faith. Therefore we must be careful but fearless as we look forward in ministering God's goodness to people. To evangelize is to seek opportunities to do the work of faith. Confidence in God is victory over fear and faithlessness. There is always hope for improvement when you are serving the living God. Those who reject God's word cannot limit His power. Peace with God takes trust; you must know that He cares for the work you do in His name. Hell is a horrifying reality. We should worry ourselves enough to motivate every bit of our God given ability to stop people from ending up in hellfire:

> *Here is the conclusion of the matter: Fear God and keep His commandment, for this is the whole duty of man.*[480]

Finally, worship of God is a basic reality in many lives, and deep thoughts about living obediently have worried both the Church and individual worshippers across all historical periods. The tie is between faithful worship and life's challenges. Based on evidence of convincing use of scripture, which this book conveys,

---

480   Eccl. 12:13

we are challenged as Christians seeking to live in faith to connect to the changes. By this understanding, you will faithfully fulfill the need for centrality of worship in a Christian life. May the Lord's grace be with you always_.